# The Education Systems of the United Kingdom

# The Education Systems of the United Kingdom

Edited by David Phillips

*Oxford Studies in Comparative Education*
*Series Editor: David Phillips*

**Symposium Books**
PO Box 65, Wallingford, Oxford OX10 0YG, United Kingdom


Published in the United Kingdom, 2000


ISBN 1 873927 73 8


This publication is also available on a subscription basis
as Volume 9(2) of *Oxford Studies in Comparative Education*
(ISSN 0961-2149)

Typeset in Monotype Plantin by Symposium Books
Printed and bound in the United Kingdom by Cambridge University Press

# Contents

# Preface

The chapters which make up this volume of *Oxford Studies in Comparative Education* attempt to describe the essential distinctive features of educational provision in the four parts of the United Kingdom. Stephen Gorard, David Matheson and Seamus Dunn have contributed chapters on Wales, Scotland and Northern Ireland respectively, while David Raffe and his colleagues provide a special case study of the unification of academic and vocational learning in Wales. David Raffe has also written an overview which serves as an introduction to the theme of the volume as a whole.

During 1999 we saw some of the most important developments for centuries in terms of devolved power in the United Kingdom, and the effects of these changes on future educational policy will be followed with great interest. The present chapters can thus be read as reflecting the situation as we begin a new era of government.

It is hoped that this volume will be of interest to comparativists within and beyond the United Kingdom, and that it will serve to convince those who are still inclined to use the term that the *British* education system does not exist!

**David Phillips**
Series Editor *Oxford Studies in Comparative Education* and
Director of the Centre for Comparative Studies in Education,
University of Oxford, United Kingdom

# Investigating the Education Systems of the United Kingdom

## DAVID RAFFE

### Introduction

A comparative researcher examining the education and training systems of the United Kingdom (UK) is likely to be struck by two features. First, in a wider international context the systems' similarities are more substantial than the differences among them. While they differ in several important respects, the education systems of England, Scotland, Wales and Northern Ireland share recognisably 'British' features. Second, the systems are politically and functionally interdependent, and shaped by common socio-economic and political factors, to a greater extent than the education systems of separate nation states.

Some researchers react to the similarity and interdependence of the UK systems by dismissing the differences among them and confining their attention to a spurious 'British' or 'UK' education system. Other researchers pay attention to the differences, but only compare them systematically within a restricted frame of reference. Most comparative studies of education and training within the UK fall into two categories. The first comprises studies of specific differences in institutions or practices in the different countries. For example, Bennett et al (1994) contrasted English, Welsh and Scottish arrangements as part of their study of the introduction of Training and Enterprise Councils (TECs) and Local Enterprise Companies (LECs); Burdin & Semple (1995) compared curricular and vocational guidance in England and Scotland; Raab et al (1997) studied the different arrangements for devolving school management in England and Scotland; and Croxford (1999) compared the impact of the different National Curriculums on gender differences. Studies of this kind are potentially of great value to policy and practice because the lessons are more likely to be transferable from one system to another (Rose, 1993). The systems and their contexts are similar; the 'other things' are more nearly 'equal'. There is considerable potential for further studies of this kind; for example, there could be useful lessons to be learnt from a comparison of funding methodologies, or of the inspection function, or of the role and organisation of Further Education (FE), in different parts of the UK.

The second and much larger category of research focuses on a single system, such as Wales or Scotland; it typically analyses the history and development of the system, or attempts to describe it for the benefit of outsiders (e.g. Clark & Munn, 1997; Gorard, 1997). This research is not overtly comparative, but England is the omnipresent reference point. The distinctive features of the system are perceived to be those which differ from England, even if the comparison is never systematic and is often implicit.

By contrast, there has been relatively little research which systematically compares the whole education system – or a substantial part of it – across the countries of the UK. The studies of this kind which have been carried out are now dated (e.g. Osborne, 1966; Bell & Grant, 1977). More recent comparisons at a system or macro level have looked overseas, rather than within the UK, for their comparator countries. However the establishment of a Scottish Parliament and Welsh Assembly with responsibility for education and training, and the re-establishment of a Northern Ireland Assembly, make this an opportune moment to re-examine the differences and similarities of the four UK systems and the relationships among them. This is my main theme in this chapter. I start by re-visiting the two features summarised above: the common Britishness (as well as the differences) of the four systems, and their interdependence. I then introduce a third feature which may also strike the comparative researcher: that the similarities and differences of the four systems, and their relations of interdependence, have changed and are continuing to change.

I illustrate this historical perspective by describing recent changes in post-compulsory education and training. The post-compulsory systems are of particularly interest, partly because they differ in interesting ways across the UK, but also because they are in a period of rapid change which may prove to be a critical phase in their historical development. Historians and sociologists typically trace the enduring characteristics of education systems to the circumstances of their emergence as national systems (Archer, 1979; Green, 1990). Over the past two decades post-compulsory education and training have expanded enormously, and they have become more functionally complex. They have had to find new principles for coherence, progression and coordination of what had previously been relatively specialised and loosely connected institutions. In other words, they are emerging as national systems. The trends described in this chapter may therefore have lasting implications for their national distinctiveness in future years.

The more specific argument of the chapter is that there has been a weakening of mutual dependence of the four systems, which may in turn increase the differences among them. There is a growing potential for divergence, but it is too soon to say whether this potential will be realised. This conclusion, albeit provisional, raises issues for theories of educational change. Recent comparative research on education systems has been strongly influenced by the tradition of 'societal analysis' associated with Maurice et al (1986), which stresses the interdependence of education and training systems with such features of the societal context as the political culture, political institutions, the economy, the labour market and industrial relations system, family structure, and so on. Recent researchers comparing educational change in different countries have concluded that despite the common problems and pressures facing most education systems there is little evidence of convergence either in the policy strategies adopted or in the direction of change actually taken by the systems (Jallade, 1989; Meijer, 1991; Ashton & Green, 1996; Green et al, 1999; Lasonen & Young, 1998). This lack of convergence among education systems is typically explained in terms of the variation in their cultural origins and societal contexts, as described above. However the cultural origins and societal contexts of the UK education systems are broadly similar – at least by comparison with systems elsewhere. If the UK systems nevertheless diverge, or demonstrate a potential for divergence, this would suggest that education systems are less determined by culture and context than the stronger versions of the societal approach would claim. Instead, current developments in post-compulsory education and training in the UK are substantially driven, or at least mediated, by internal pressures within each system; and these systems are sufficiently different for each to generate its own distinct momentum and direction of change.

### Differences and Similarities

Some of the differences among the four systems are substantial, in the sense that they relate to what may be seen as system-defining characteristics. These include:

- the organisation of secondary education, which in Northern Ireland is still selective (Wilson, 1987), whereas Scotland, Wales and (a little more equivocally) England are comprehensive. If the amount of energy devoted by researchers and policy commentators to selective secondary schooling is any indication, this difference is sociologically and educationally very significant;
- the philosophy underlying the curriculum (Harrison, 1997). In England, Wales and Northern Ireland there is a statutory subject-based National Curriculum from the age of five; the details of the prescribed curriculum vary across the three territories, but not the underlying principles. In Scotland the curriculum from 5 to 14 is based on five broad curriculum areas, and from 14 to 16 on eight 'modes' of study (Croxford, 1999). In practice, the differences are more pronounced in primary than secondary schools, where subjects dominate the curriculum in Scotland as they do elsewhere. A further curricular difference is found in post-compulsory and

higher education, where the Scottish system offers a broader curriculum, at least in principle;

- modularity and tracking in post-16 courses and qualifications. Again, the principal difference is between Scotland, where the curriculum comprises shorter academic courses (Highers) and vocational modules, and the rest of the UK where it comprises longer academic courses (A Levels) and vocational programmes leading to group awards. Partly as a result, the distinction between post-16 tracks are weaker in Scotland than elsewhere (Raffe, 1993). In a recent project, we identified a continuum from 'tracked' to 'unified' systems of post-compulsory education: the English and Welsh systems represent 'tracked' systems and the Scottish system an intermediate 'linked' system, although all three countries are moving along this continuum in the direction of a more unified system (Spours et al, 1998a; see Raffe et al elsewhere in this book).

However most of the differences among the UK systems are more modest. These include differences in arrangements for parental choice of school, in the local management of schools, in the funding of further and higher education, in the organisation of the inspection function, in the training and registration of teachers, and so on. In other words, most of the differences are of the kind discussed above, which may be the subject of applied comparative research looking for transferable policies and practices. In these cases the systems incorporate broadly similar educational and policy aims, which are pursued through somewhat different institutions or arrangements.

Expressed more positively, the systems share common 'British' characteristics. Green et al (1999, pp. 26–27) note that education systems can be grouped into regionally-based types. They place the UK systems in the same type, whether this is identified on the basis of common cultural influences (liberalism, philosophical empiricism and traditions of knowledge specialisation and individualised, child-centred pedagogy) or of principles of organisation (*laissez-faire* liberal traditions with weak forms of organised social partnership, associated with voluntarism and local autonomy). Compared with other European countries the UK systems share a strong emphasis on market principles and concepts of flexibility. Post-compulsory education and training in the UK is distinctive as a 'mixed model' (see below). In a recent paper colleagues and I drew attention to 'a distinctively British pattern of participation in education and training, characterised by relatively high proportions leaving full-time education at 16 or 17, high participation in work-based training, high participation in higher education matched by very low participation beyond 18 in intermediate-level education, and a tradition of second-chance education through part-time study .... All of these features are common to the whole UK' (Raffe et al, 1999, p. 16).

### Interdependence and Common Determinants

The common characteristics of the UK systems partly reflect their interdependence and the extent to which they are shaped by the same economic and social contextual features. There are at least three aspects of this interdependence.

The first and perhaps the most obvious is political interdependence. The four systems belong to the same nation state. Except for the period up to 1972 when the Stormont Parliament was responsible for education in Northern Ireland, the four systems have all been subject to the same Parliament at Westminster. Of course, common political control has not necessarily meant uniformity of policy. Policy-makers in Scotland and (more recently) Wales have developed considerable skills in exploiting their freedom of manoeuvre to pursue policies which diverged from those of England (Jones, 1997; Raffe, 1998). Nevertheless this freedom has been constrained by the need to justify divergent policies in terms of a rhetoric of 'adapting UK policy to local circumstances'. And Scotland, Wales and Northern Ireland have frequently been compelled to adopt policies introduced to address political problems internal to England. Often, as in the case of many of the Conservative government's curbs on local authority power, these policies have addressed the political problems of the south-eastern corner of England (Ball, 1997).

The political interdependence of the four systems may sometimes generate political pressures for divergence rather than for uniformity. Within each territory there is a subtle political discourse of similarity and distinctiveness. Especially in Wales and Scotland, the perception that a policy is nationally distinctive and not 'anglicising' may be as important for its political appeal as its more intrinsic merits or demerits (Bellin et al, 1994). Policy-makers may therefore seek to differentiate policy within their territory, although this often leads to changes in nomenclature and 'badging' rather than more substantial differences in policy or in institutions.

The second aspect is the functional interdependence of the four systems. There are large flows of students between the four systems, especially at higher education level. A substantial proportion of school leavers from Northern Ireland who enter higher education, and about half of those from Wales, do so in a different part of the UK (Cormack et al, 1997; Rees & Istance, 1997). There are significant, if more constrained, flows of teachers. In all the British education systems qualifications play important roles, including goal-setting, regulation and articulation; the main qualifications are the same throughout the UK, except for Scotland, and even Scottish qualifications must be compatible with those elsewhere in the UK (and they face competition from awarding bodies in England). There are also flows of ideas and policies between the UK systems. Wales, Northern Ireland and to a lesser extent Scotland are reliant on the policy-making capacity of England.

Within each territory the number of civil servants and professionals able to develop new policies is severely limited; England plays the lead role in policy development and policy-makers elsewhere need to 'pick and choose' the areas where separate policy development is required (Raffe, 1998).

Finally, each education system is located within, and partly shaped by, a social and economic context which is relatively homogeneous throughout the UK. For example, the main structures of the labour market are British or UK-wide in scope (Ashton, 1988). There is a strong pressure for common occupational standards and qualifications. Key stakeholders, including industry and training organisations tend to be organised at a UK level. The social processes within education, and the individual orientations to education, appear to be similar (Raffe et al, 1999). For example, where participation patterns differ this reflects differences in institutional arrangements and opportunities, rather than differences in individual values or orientations to education (Gray et al, 1992).

## Common Trends in Post-Compulsory Education and Training

Neither the similarities and differences of the four systems, nor their relations of mutual dependence, are frozen in time. The four systems have been evolving in relation to each other, and this process may now have reached a critical phase. In the rest of this chapter I discuss these trends in relation to post-compulsory education and training; for reasons of data I focus mainly on England, Scotland and Wales. I start by describing some common features, and trends, in the four systems.

Each system may be represented – at least heuristically – as having an academic track, a broad vocational track and a work-based track. The principal courses in the academic track have led to Highers in Scotland and to A Levels elsewhere. The second track comprises full-time courses in broad occupational areas, such as BTEC Diplomas and General National Vocational Qualifications (GNVQs) in England and Wales. In Scotland this track until recently comprised National Certificate modules (often grouped into General Scottish Vocational Qualifications [GSVQ] or other group awards). However, in 1999 modules and GSVQs were brought, along with Highers, into a unified system of post-16 courses and qualifications. The third track comprises work-based youth training programmes leading to occupational qualifications (NVQs and SVQs). The structure of tracks varies across the systems: courses and qualifications are more modular in Scotland and the divisions between tracks are somewhat weaker. All the systems share a distinctively British characteristic: that it is possible to map the system either in terms of qualifications or in terms of institutions, and the two maps do not precisely coincide. Academic courses tend to be offered in schools and vocational courses in colleges of FE, but the relationship between qualifications and institutions is not precise, and varies locally. As an added complication, there is much greater institutional variability in England (and to a lesser extent Wales) where there are more categories of schools and FE colleges (including Sixth Form and Tertiary colleges). Occupational qualifications are primarily offered on the work-based programme formerly called Youth Training, but they may be delivered through part-time and sometimes full-time programmes in FE colleges.

In the 1980s, the Organisation for Economic Co-operation and Development (OECD, 1985) identified 'three different approaches or models of provision at the post-compulsory level' (p. 47). The schooling model, exemplified by the USA, Japan and Sweden, relied mainly on schools to deliver education, including vocational education, at this level. The dual model, exemplified by the German-speaking countries, provided much vocational education and training at this level through a well-established apprenticeship system. The 'mixed or pluralist' model, exemplified by the UK, was characterised by the greater importance of the 'non-formal sector' of youth training schemes as distinct from the school (and college) sector and from institutionalised apprenticeships. The mixed model was 'more commonly found in countries where schools represent the dominant form of provision and where the potential for growth at the post-compulsory level is still relatively high' (p. 47). 'Policies aimed at the development of such a model ... essentially favour the development of separate initial training schemes outside schools or clearly distinct from programmes provided within the formal sector' (p. 47). The UK government's New Training Initiative of 1981 aimed to focus the expansion of post-compulsory provision on the Youth Training Scheme (YTS) which it was then preparing to introduce, rather than on full-time education (Manpower Services Commission [MSC], 1981).

YTS quickly became a mass training scheme and in the late 1980s it catered for nearly four in 10 of the age group, although some of these did not stay on it for long. However it did not achieve the ambitious goals of the New Training Initiative; it inherited low status from the unemployment schemes it replaced, and it failed to acquire a reputation for quality training (Raffe et al, 1998a). The number of trainees fell rapidly when participation in full-time education began to rise steeply in the late 1980s. Nevertheless the successors of YTS continue as distinctive features of the British educational scene.

The most significant trend of the last decade has been the growth in full-time participation. The proportion of 16-year-olds continuing in full-time education rose from less than 50% in the mid 1980s to nearly 75% in the mid 1990s. (It subsequently fell very slightly.) The proportion of the age group entering full-time higher education doubled over a similar period, to reach 33% in 1996/97 (Department for Education and Employment [DfEE], 1998: GB figures). Nevertheless some distinctively British features of participation have persisted, notably a rapid falling-off in participation by age and a relatively low rate of participation beyond 18 years except in higher education.

A further trend that is common to the UK systems is the policy drive to 'unify' post-compulsory education and training: that is, to reduce divisions between academic and vocational tracks and to develop a more coherent system. The concept of 'unification' is discussed in Raffe et al later in this book. New governmental, advisory, regulatory and qualifications bodies have been created to cover both academic and vocational tracks, often by merging bodies specific to one track. The most prominent examples are the DfEE and the Scottish Office Education and Industry Department (SOEID) – since replaced by the departments of the Scottish Executive – in Scotland (Spours et al, 1998b). Another instrument of unification is the development of unified qualifications or qualifications frameworks covering academic and vocational subjects. These policy developments reflect two further trends which are characteristically British: the use of qualifications to drive change, and the growing reliance upon monitoring, regulation and quality assurance procedures to control and regulate a flexible and diverse system.

The final common trend is that educational change in general, and policy-led change in particular, has responded to internal problems of the education and training system much more than to new demands or needs arising from external changes. This is not to deny that external factors have been important drivers of change. For example the increase in participation is partly attributable to socio-demographic trends which have increased the proportion of the age group from family backgrounds conducive to high participation. It is also partly attributable to labour-market changes which have reduced opportunities for early leavers and increased opportunities and rewards for graduates and those with qualifications from post-compulsory education. Labour-market changes, and especially the decline in craft occupations, also help to explain the relative failure of the work-based route and the mixed model strategy that was built on it. The drive for unification can be attributed, at least indirectly, to economic globalisation and the associated drive for 'competitiveness', to the demands for higher levels and new kinds of attainment, and to pressures arising from social and economic inequality and the increased risk of social exclusion (Raffe et al, 1998b).

However to a large extent change has been driven by factors internal to the education system; or where the sources of change are external they have been mediated by the education system itself. For example, the growth in participation at 16-plus was at least partly the result of increased opportunities in higher education and of reforms to compulsory education which gave 16-year-olds a more positive attitude to continued education and higher attainments on which to build. Once the process of educational expansion had started, with the consequent increase in the functional complexity of the system, it generated its own dynamic and momentum for further change. Expansion exposed the inadequacies of existing provision in catering for, and motivating, a broader and more diverse range of students. It exposed cul-de-sacs and weaknesses in existing progression opportunities. It exposed, and exacerbated, the low status of vocational education. It made it necessary to rationalise educational provision, to improve coherence and coordination, to maintain consistency in standards, to optimise resource allocation to different parts of system, and so on. In short, it created pressures for unification within post-compulsory education and training systems.

However countries within the UK – and beyond it – have responded with different strategies for unification (Spours et al, 1998a). And even where change has been less directly policy-led similar pressures have resulted in different outcomes within each system. For example the expansion of participation resulted in a very different balance of academic and vocational courses in Scotland and England, a consequence of their different course structures as described below. And the problems raised by expansion are manifested in different pressure points within each system: as inadequate provision for 'middle attainers' and problems of progression in Scotland, as problems of 'standards' and 'breadth' in England, as problems of participation and access in Wales.

Moreover, each system's response to the pressures for change depends on the composition, values and perceived interests of its policy community. This is a further source of possible divergence. The composition of the policy community varies across the territories: for example, independent schools are more numerous and more influential in England than in Wales or Scotland. Values may differ: for example there is stronger commitment to collective values in education (and a stronger rejection of tracking) in Scotland than elsewhere (Howieson et al, 1997). In our review of similarities and differences across the UK systems we concluded that the cultural differences affecting *individual* behaviour within education – such as the decision to participate – were relatively small, but that there were stronger differences in *collective* values about the politics and organisation of the education system itself (Raffe et al, 1999). Many members of the policy community have a direct interest in the autonomy of their system as this is the basis of their own power and influence. They have a further interest in differentiating their system from other UK systems. In the words of one policy-maker, 'we can only have it under our control if we're different' (quoted in Raffe, 1998, p. 598).

In other words, even if many of the factors driving educational change are common to the UK systems, they are mediated by factors internal to each system; and the systems and their internal political structures are sufficiently different to generate a different momentum and direction of change within each system. Divergence is therefore possible. But is it happening? I examine the evidence in the next section.

## Different or Divergent Trends in
## Post-Compulsory Education and Training

There is not space here for a detailed comparison of recent trends in UK post-compulsory education and training systems; for a fuller account of England and Scotland see Howieson et al, (1997). Here I simply list seven examples of different or divergent trends. Individually, each trend is modest; collectively, they add up to an increased potential for divergence across the four systems.

1. *Increase in full-time participation.* The increase in participation beyond 16 has not been parallel across the UK. Unfortunately the different statistical sources tell inconsistent stories about trends in participation. According to government statistics, in 1986/87 the participation rate at 16 years was 57% in Scotland and 47% in England. Thereafter participation rose more rapidly in England and by 1993/94 the rate was 73% in both countries. However, participation continued to rise in Scotland, to a rate of 80% in 1997/98, while it fell back in England to a low point of 69% in the same year. The Welsh trend has been closer to that in England; figures for Northern Ireland do not cover trends over a comparable period. These trends are based on official statistics reported by the DfEE (1999) and the Scottish Executive (1999). Other sources, such as the England and Wales Youth Cohort Survey (YCS) and the Scottish Young Peoples Survey and Scottish School Leavers Survey (SYPS/SSLS), reveal a smaller relative increase in Scottish participation during the 1990s.

These trends suggest that the dynamics of growth in participation have been different. It is not easy to explain the difference. A possible explanation for the faster growth in England and Wales before 1993 is the recession of the early 1990s, which was widely believed to encourage participation in education, and which was significantly deeper in parts of England and Wales than in Scotland. However participation rates began to accelerate in the late 1980s when the labour market was still very tight, and cross-sectional studies have failed to find a link between unemployment and participation in England and Wales (Gray et al, 1992). A second possible explanation is that England and Wales had more appropriate courses to offer the additional students who stayed on; I discuss this further below. A third possible explanation is that young people in England and Wales were encouraged to participate as schools and colleges vigorously promoted post-16 opportunities in the competitive education market established by the Conservative government; competition at 16-plus has been less significant in Scotland because the system does not provide a significant break at 16 and most stayers continue at the same school. If either of the last two explanations is valid, this would mean that the different trends in participation were the result of differences in the education systems.

2. *Modularisation.* In England moves towards a more modular course structure have been patchy and limited in scope. Successive attempts to reform A Levels in the 1980s and early 1990s were resisted. 'Vertical' AS Levels were introduced, equivalent to half an A Level, but their take-up was low. Modular A Levels were introduced in the 1990s but have remained controversial, especially among those who feared that frequent re-sits would mean a decline in standards. A Levels have tended to remain an all-or-nothing qualification: a majority of students taking A Levels have taken a full diet of three or four. The main vocational courses, BTECs and GNVQs, have been group awards. While Wales used the same courses and qualifications as England it went further down the road towards modularisation and credit-rating, notably in FE where the Welsh Credit Framework has covered 90% of the curriculum.

In Scotland, by contrast, the curriculum has developed on a more modular basis. In 1984 the modular National Certificate (NC) replaced non-advanced vocational education in colleges and schools. The NC covered full-time and work-based provision and allowed them to be better articulated, although this benefit was partly lost after 1989 when Scotland was required to introduce occupational SVQs on the same model as English NVQs; many SVQs were based not on NC modules but on new workplace-assessed units. Together with the semi-modular Scottish Higher the NC provided a basis for mixing academic and vocational subjects within the secondary school, and therefore resulted in a relatively weak distinction between academic and vocational tracks in full-time education. The introduction of the NC was an important milestone in the development of the Scottish system and in its divergence from the English system. In some respects this was its purpose: it was an attempt by the Scottish policy community to maintain control in the face of encroachments from the Manpower Services Commission, whose remit covered the whole of Britain.

The modularity, or lack of modularity, of an education system is a powerful determinant of how it responds to future pressures for change. A modular course structure has helped Scotland to adapt and innovate in a smoother and more incremental way than England, where change has proceeded less steadily through fits and starts. One example is the attempt to 'vocationalise' the secondary curriculum through the Technical and Vocational Education Initiative (TVEI) (Bell et al, 1989). Scotland was able to integrate TVEI more fully into mainstream practice than England where it more often formed a separate enclave within education and where many of the innovations it had inspired were reversed when the National Curriculum was introduced.

3. *Growth of the broad vocational (middle) track.* However, a modular course structure may have less positive consequences, and it may have made it harder for Scotland to withstand the pressures of 'academic drift'. England

and Wales have developed a substantial full-time vocational track which has catered for many of the additional students produced by the growth in participation; the existing course structure in Scotland has made it difficult for such a track to emerge.

BTEC, GNVQ and other vocational group awards have developed as a large and relatively distinctive middle track in England and Wales. These programmes found a clear constituency among the extra stayers-on for whom a programme of three A Levels was not a realistic prospect. By 1996 three out of seven students aged 16-plus in full-time education in England were taking vocational programmes, with a similar proportion in Wales (DfEE, 1997). In Scotland the more modular course structure meant that the equivalent students had easier access at least to a restricted form of the academic track; that is, they could take one or two Highers, mixed with NC modules, with the possibility of taking further Highers in the second post-compulsory year. Although GSVQs were introduced at the same time as GNVQs in England, with broadly similar objectives, they comprised whole programmes which could not easily be combined with Highers. They did not provide a counter-attraction to the higher-status alternative of Highers and failed to develop a clear constituency. They were attempted by a relatively small proportion of the age group; most GSVQ students were based in college, and they were typically less-qualified than GNVQ students in England or Wales. Full-time FE provision at 16- and 17-plus in Scotland has been much smaller and lower in status than in England and Wales.

4. *Development of the work-based route.* YTS, introduced by the MSC in 1983, was a British-wide scheme with few variations in Wales or Scotland except for those made necessary by different school-leaving arrangements or by the introduction of Scottish NC modules. However the measures that replaced it have increasingly been organised on a different basis in England, Wales and Scotland.

YTS and its successors struggled to escape the vicious circle of low status, perceived low quality, under-investment by employers and under-regulation. After several changes during the 1980s, YTS was replaced in 1990 by Youth Training (YT) and control was passed to the TECs in England and Wales and to LECs in Scotland. YT was more employer-led and more flexible in its specification of 'inputs' such as the duration and form of training; it was controlled and funded mainly through 'outputs' in the form of qualifications. There was a brief experiment with Youth Credits in the early 1990s – designed to bring training closer to employment and to increase young people's 'ownership' of their skills – and in 1994 the first Modern Apprenticeships were introduced. Modern Apprenticeships were designed to increase the status of work-based training by offering training at level 3 (equivalent to A Level), closely tailored to the needs of employers, incorporating core skills. National Traineeships, first introduced in 1997, incorporate many of the features of Modern Apprenticeships but at level 2. In

England a three-tier system is now emerging, based on Modern Apprenticeships, National Traineeships and a third level of provision which is still to be defined. In principle the status of youth training will be a function of the level of qualification and there will be a progression route linking the levels. A similar system is emerging in Wales. The main differences between England and Wales are differences of emphasis: Wales has attached more importance than England to Modern Apprenticeships, especially in engineering, to complement the country's economic development strategy.

Scottish arrangements for Youth Training began to diverge in 1990 when control passed to LECs. Unlike the English and Welsh TECs, the LECs were coordinated by central bodies: Scottish Enterprise and Highland and Islands Enterprise. Skillseekers, the Scottish version of Youth Credits phased in between 1991–96, are perceived to have been more effective than their English equivalents, partly because of the greater national coordination and partly because of more effective partnership with employers. Modern Apprenticeships have been incorporated within Skillseekers and National Traineeships have not been introduced in Scotland. There thus remains a single-tier framework for youth training in Scotland in contrast with the three-tier system south of the Border.

Youth Training in Northern Ireland has always been separate from that in the rest of Britain. Its Youth Training Programme (YTP) was introduced in 1982, one year ahead of the YTS which it resembled. In 1995, following local pilots, the YTP was replaced by the Jobskills programme. Many features of Jobskills reflect current trends in youth training elsewhere in the UK: it emphasises NVQs, with a performance-related element in funding; it provides training at NVQ levels 1, 2 and 3; it seeks to give trainees 'ownership' through a training credit; and it guarantees places for 16- and 17-year-old school-leavers who want them. However it covers a wider age band (first-time entrants to the labour market up to 24 years, and unemployed people up to 60 years), and it offers a broader training, including core skills, than most British schemes at the time of its introduction (Training and Employment Agency, n.d.).

Thus, different arrangements for work-based training are emerging in the different parts of the UK. While none of the differences is radical, they suggest that each system has acquired its own momentum for further development, with the possibility of further divergence.

5. *Strategies for post-16 reform.* England, Wales and Scotland are pursuing different strategies for the unification of post-compulsory education and training (Spours et al, 1998a). England and Wales are pursuing 'linkages' strategies to develop links between the different tracks; the strategy in Scotland is to replace the tracks with a unified system, under the Higher Still reforms. The contrast between these strategies is discussed further in a later chapter. There is a further policy difference. In England there are distinct policy agendas for the 16–19 age group and for older adults, with the former

dominated by school-related concerns with breadth and standards; in Wales and Scotland policies for 16–19-year-olds are more influenced by the lifelong learning agenda of access, participation and flexibility. In England there is reluctance to allow 16–19-year-olds to participate fully in any future credit accumulation system; in Wales and Scotland current efforts to develop credit and qualifications frameworks are already in progress, and cover all potential learners from age 16 upwards.

There are several reasons for these different approaches. Each country is attempting to build on what are perceived to be the strengths of its existing system. In Scotland these strengths include the existing flexibility and modularity of the system; in Wales they include the achievements of reforms such as the Credit Framework. In England the reputation of the A Level is perceived, at least by some, to be a strength. At the same time, each country is seeking to reverse the corresponding weaknesses of the system, namely the problems of coherence in a flexible system in Scotland, the lack of breadth in England, and so on. In addition, the different strategies reflect the different cultures and priorities of the education policy community in each system: notably the political reluctance to challenge the A Level in England, and the resistance to tracking in Scotland.

6. *Administrative devolution.* Parallel to the changes described above, and pre-dating the political devolution of 1999, there was a process of devolution of administrative responsibilities to the Scottish and Welsh Offices and to the Department of Education and other agencies in Northern Ireland. These changes followed a different pattern and timetable within each territory. Northern Ireland has had devolved responsibilities for most aspects of education and training since the province was partitioned from the rest of Ireland in 1921. The Scottish Office had had responsibility for schools and colleges since 1885, but higher education and training were devolved more recently, in 1992 and 1994 respectively. The administration and control of Welsh education were almost fully integrated with English education until 1970, but by 1999 they were largely separate. In each territory separate 'quangos' have been established with regulatory, advisory, quality, funding and other functions.

These trends may be traced to the interaction of at least three sets of factors. The first is the desire of policy communities within each system to increase their power, supported (at least within Scotland and Wales) by popular approval for the greater devolution of policy-making. The second factor is the pressure for unification discussed earlier. As each education system has grown in functional complexity it requires a more unified style of government and regulation, which is not possible if parts of the system are controlled from within the territory while other parts are controlled from London. For example, school and college education have become increasingly interdependent with training on the one hand and with universities on the other; before 1992 this made it increasingly difficult to coordinate policy within either Scotland or Wales, where schools and colleges were controlled by the Scottish or Welsh Office but training and universities were controlled by London Departments. It was not politically possible to take control of schools and colleges away from the Scottish and Welsh Offices; the logical solution was therefore to give them control of training and universities as well. A similar logic, at a more detailed level, led to the creation of new quangos within each territory. The third factor is the reduction in the powers of local government and the increased centralisation of power, especially during the 1980s. Although this was initially an English phenomenon it had implications for the other UK systems. As Jones (1997, p. 154) notes: 'From a Welsh point of view this reassertion of power at the centre was of enormous import because it was accompanied by a greater devolution of power to the Welsh Office than had ever previously been the case'.

The implications for possible divergence are evident. Not only does each territory have an increased power and – to some extent – capacity for separate policy-making, but the nature of policy-making is likely to vary. The various agencies that have been established within each system tend not to be parallel; that is, they tend to differ in their organisation, scope and functions (Raffe et al, 1999). Not only do policy-makers increasingly interact with other policy-makers within the same territory, rather than in other parts of the UK, but the nature of these interactions will be different, over and above the effects of differences in scale and in politics. As the nature of policy-making varies, so may its outcomes.

7. *Political devolution.* Finally, from 1999 there has been a Scottish Parliament and Assemblies in Wales and Northern Ireland, all with responsibility for education and training (but without legislative powers in the case of Wales). Administrative devolution will be matched by political devolution.

## Are the Systems Diverging?

The changes documented above point to a reduction in the interdependence of the UK systems. Earlier in the chapter I described three aspects of interdependence: political interdependence, functional interdependence and a shared social and economic context. Political interdependence is being reduced by administrative and political devolution. The functional interdependence of the systems is less directly affected by the changes described above, but each system may be better able to negotiate the terms of this interdependence, and at least one aspect of functional interdependence is being directly reduced by devolution as each system develops an enhanced capacity for separate policy-making. With respect to the societal context of education, the growth in participation in education has reduced the homogenising constraining influence of the UK labour market on compulsory education and the immediate post-compulsory stage. Finally, devolution may encourage the further development of distinct political cultures.

It remains to be seen whether this will lead to significant divergence among the systems. They are currently pursuing different strategies, but any conclusions about convergence or divergence depend on the dimensions of change that are examined and the period of time (Spours et al, 1998a). If the different strategies are seen as different steps in a longer-term process, in which some countries are more advanced than others, they may well lead to future convergence (Spours & Young, 1996). Furthermore, there is no necessary connection between political devolution and system divergence. Education in Northern Ireland drew closer to the English system at a time when it was controlled by a separate Parliament (Bell & Grant, 1977); conversely, Welsh education diverged while it remained under the control of Westminster. A democratically elected parliament or assembly may feel under less pressure to assert its legitimacy by promoting national distinctiveness than the Scottish and Welsh Offices appeared to feel. And the power of professionals and civil servants, with vested interest in distinctiveness, will be reduced.

It is possible that the pattern of convergence and divergence may be uneven across systems or parts of the system. For example some policy-makers have speculated that the Welsh and English systems may diverge but the English and Scottish systems will converge; and it is possible that there will be convergence in some areas, perhaps in qualifications frameworks and technology-led developments, with divergence in other areas such as school organisation.

On balance, I conclude that the potential for divergence will at least partly be realised. One of my main arguments in this chapter is that education systems can develop their own momentum and direction of change, partly independent of any broader socio-economic forces driving change, and that relatively small differences in systems can have important implications for their future development. Divergence may come about, as it were, by accident. This will be even more likely if each system develops its separate capacity for policy-making. Even before political devolution, UK policy-makers paid little attention to policy developments in the other UK systems unless they were compelled to (Raffe, 1998); policies and systems may simply drift apart if there are no strong and tangible pressures to keep them together. The UK systems, perhaps, resemble parallel rivers flowing across a plain. The strength of their flow is similar, and so is the gradient and geological structure of the land through which they pass, but a few randomly scattered boulders could produce wide variations in the directions in which they move.

**Conclusion**

My discussion points to at least three precepts for comparative research on the education systems of the UK. First, such research needs to compare them *as systems*, or at least to locate more detailed comparisons within a broader system frame of reference. This frame of reference has been sadly absent from recent research. Second, the research needs to take account of the *interdependence* of the UK systems, and to treat this as an object of study. A study which simply places the systems side by side, as if autonomous and unconnected, will miss important truths whatever its analytical framework. Third, the research needs a *historical perspective*, and to take account of the fact that the systems and the relationships among them are constantly changing.

I have illustrated these precepts by discussing the development of post-compulsory education and training since the early 1980s. The trends during this period indicate a weakening of interdependence, and a potential for divergence among the systems. It remains to be seen whether this potential will be realised, but I have suggested that this has been a critical period in the development of these systems; political devolution makes it even more critical.

Finally, this chapter has demonstrated the potential of comparisons within the UK to inform wider theoretical debates. Much comparative research – and especially in post-compulsory education – continues to be strongly influenced by the societal approach. Comparisons within a nation state such as the UK provide an interesting test of many of the assumptions of this approach, for example about the boundaries of systems and internal variation within these boundaries (Raffe et al, 1999). The argument of this chapter, that education systems may diverge even within a similar societal context, provides a reminder that education systems may not be tightly determined by their contexts and that change may be driven more by the internal dynamics of the systems themselves.

*Acknowledgements*

This chapter is a product of the Home Internationals Project (A 'Home Internationals' Comparison of 14–19 Education and Training Systems in the UK), funded by the Economic and Research Council in the Centre for Educational Sociology, University of Edinburgh (R000236840). The contribution of colleagues on the project, Linda Croxford, Chris Martin and Karen Brannen, is gratefully acknowledged. The chapter draws on a seminar given at the Department of Educational Studies, University of Oxford in October 1998, and benefits from comments and discussion with seminar participants.

## References

Archer, M. (1979) *The Social Origin of Education Systems.* London: Sage.

Ashton, D. (1988) Educational Institutions, Youth and the Labour Market, in D. Gallie (Ed.) *Employment in Britain.* Oxford: Blackwell.

Ashton, D. & Green, F. (1996) *Education, Training and the Global Economy.* Cheltenham: Edward Elgar.

Ball, S. (1997) The Englishness of English Education Policy: a research agenda, paper presented to British Educational Research Association (BERA) symposium on 'A Disunited Kingdom?', September, York (King's College London).

Bell, C., Howieson, K., King, K. & Raffe, D. (1989) The Scottish Dimension of TVEI, in A. Brown & D. McCrone (Eds) *The Scottish Government Yearbook 1989.* Edinburgh: Unit for the Study of Government in Scotland, University of Edinburgh.

Bell, R. & Grant, N. (1977) *Patterns of Education in the British Isles.* London: George Allen & Unwin.

Bellin, W., Osmond, J. & Reynolds, D. (1994) *Towards an Educational Policy for Wales.* Cardiff: Institute for Welsh Affairs.

Bennett, R., Wicks, P. & McCoshan, A. (1994) *Local Empowerment and Business Services: Britain's experiment with Training and Enterprise Councils.* London: UCL Press.

Burdin, J. & Semple, S. (1995) *Guidance for Learning and Work: report of an Anglo-Scottish Consultation.* Glasgow: CRAC, NICEC and University of Strathclyde.

Clark, M. & Munn, P. (Eds) (1997) *Education in Scotland: Policy and practice from pre-school to secondary.* London: Routledge.

Cormack, R., Gallagher, A. & Osborne, R. (1997) Higher Education Participation in Northern Ireland, *Higher Education Quarterly,* 51, pp. 68–85.

Croxford, L. (1999) Gender and National Curricula, in J. Salisbury & S. Riddell (Eds) *Gender, Policy and Educational Change.* London: Routledge.

Department for Education and Employment (DfEE) (1997) *Participation in Education and Training by 16–18 Year Olds in England: 1986 to 1996.* News Release. London: DfEE.

DfEE (1998) *Departmental Report.* London: DfEE.

DfEE (1999) *Participation in Education and Training by 16–18 Year Olds in England: 1988–1998.* London: DfEE.

Gorard, S. (1997) *A Brief History of Education and Training in Wales, 1900–1996. Working Paper 4, Project on Patterns of Participation in Adult Education and Training.* Cardiff: University of Wales, Cardiff.

Gray, J., Jesson, D. & Sime, N. (1992) The 'Discouraged Worker' Revisited, *Sociology,* 26, pp. 493–505.

Green, A. (1990) *Education and State Formation: the rise of education systems in England, France and the USA.* Basingstoke: Macmillan.

Green, A., Wolf, A. & Leney, T. (1999) *Convergence and Divergence in European Education and Training Systems,* Bedford Way Papers. London: University of London Institute of Education.

Harrison, C. (1997) How Scottish is the Scottish Curriculum? in M. Clark & P. Munn (Eds) *Education in Scotland: policy and practice from pre-school to secondary*. London: Routledge.

Howieson, C., Raffe, D., Spours, K. & Young, M. (1997) Unifying Academic and Vocational Learning: the state of the debate in England and Scotland, *Journal of Education and Work*, 10, pp. 5–35.

Jallade, J-P. (1989) Recent Trends in Vocational Education and Training: an overview, *European Journal of Education*, 24, pp. 103–125.

Jones, G. (1997) *The Education of a Nation*. Cardiff: University of Wales Press.

Lasonen, J. & Young, M. (1998) *Strategies for Achieving Parity of Esteem in European Upper Secondary Education*. Jyväskylä: Institute for Educational Research, University of Jyväskylä.

Manpower Services Commission (MSC) (1981) *New Training Initiative: an agenda for action*. Sheffield: MSC.

Maurice, M., Sellier, F. & Silvestre, J-J. (1986) *The Social Foundations of Industrial Power*. Cambridge: MIT Press.

Meijer, K. (1991) Reforms in Vocational Education and Training in Italy, Spain and Portugal: similar objectives, different strategies, *European Journal of Education*, 26, pp. 13–27.

Organisation for Economic Co-operation and Development (OECD) (1985) *Education and Training after Basic Schooling*. Paris: OECD.

Osborne, G. (1966) *Scottish and English Schools: a comparative study of the past fifty years*. London: Longman.

Raab, C.D., Munn, P., McAvoy, L., Bailey, L., Arnott, M. & Adler, M. (1997) Devolving the Management of Schools in Britain, *Educational Administration Quarterly*, 33, pp. 40–157.

Raffe, D. (1993) Modular Strategies for Overcoming Academic/Vocational Divisions: issues arising from the Scottish experience, *Journal of Education Policy*, 9, pp. 141–154.

Raffe, D. (1998) Does Learning begin at Home? The Use of 'Home International' Comparisons in UK Policy-making *Journal of Education Policy*, 13, pp. 591–602.

Raffe, D., Biggart, A., Fairgrieve, J., Howieson, C., Rodger, J. & Burniston, S. (1998a) *OECD Thematic Review. The Transition from Initial Education to Working Life: UK background report*. Edinburgh: Centre for Educational Sociology, University of Edinburgh.

Raffe, D., Howieson, C., Spours, K. & Young, M. (1998b) The Unification of Post-compulsory Education: towards a conceptual framework, *British Journal of Educational Studies*, 46, pp. 169–187.

Raffe, D., Brannen, K., Croxford, L. & Martin, C. (1999) Comparing England, Scotland, Wales and Northern Ireland: the case for 'home internationals' in comparative research, *Comparative Education*, 35, pp. 9–25.

Rees, G. & Istance, D. (1997) Higher Education in Wales: the (re-)emergence of a national system? *Higher Education Quarterly*, 51, pp. 49–67.

Rose, R. (1993) *Lesson-Drawing in Public Policy: a guide to learning across time and space*. Chatham: Chatham House.

Scottish Executive (1999) *Participation in Education by 16–21 Year Olds in Scotland, 1987/88 to 1997/98*. Statistical Bulletin Edn/C3/1999/2. Edinburgh: Scottish Executive.

Spours, K., Young, M., Howieson, C. & Raffe, D. (1998a) *Unifying Academic and Vocational Learning: conclusions of the Unified Learning Project, ULP Working Paper 11*. Edinburgh: Universities of Edinburgh and London.

Spours, K., Young, M., Howieson, C. & Raffe, D. (1998b) *Regulatory and Awarding Bodies and the Process of Unification in England and Scotland, ULP Working Paper 4*. Edinburgh: Universities of Edinburgh and London).

Training and Employment Agency (n.d.) *Jobskills: your future in your hands*. Belfast: Training and Employment Agency.

Wilson, J. (1987) Selection for Secondary Education, in R. Osborne, R. Cormack & R. Miller (Eds) *Education and Policy in Northern Ireland*. Belfast: Policy Research Institute.

---

# For England, See Wales

## STEPHEN GORARD

### Introduction

This chapter initially describes differences between Wales and England in terms of structural factors, and the educational processes affected by them. In this way, and in the light of the new Assembly, it is clear that educational policy in Wales is devolving from England. The chapter then discusses some recent research findings from Wales which have led to markedly different results to the consensus from studies in England. However, when considered in terms of the methods used, some of these differences disappear, thereby suggesting that research in Wales still has considerable relevance for practitioners and policy-makers in England.

### How is Wales Different from England?

*General Differences*

Wales is clearly different to England in terms of population. Until 1995 Wales had eight Local Education Authorities (LEAs), while England had 109, any two of which (e.g. Hampshire and Essex) might have a population in excess of the whole of Wales. Even though Wales is also much smaller in area than England, its population density is minimal by comparison. The least densely populated LEA in England is Northumberland and even that is three times as densely populated as Powys in Wales. The most densely populated LEA in England, Kensington, is over 12 times as dense as South Glamorgan (Cardiff). The average population density in Wales is only 1.4 persons per hectare, compared to 2.4 for Britain as a whole. Much of Wales is still predominantly rural in nature, particularly Gwynedd, Powys, and Dyfed (apart from the Llanelli area), where the density can be as low as 0.2 persons per hectare. Only 12 towns in these three counties have a population exceeding 5,000, and transport facilities are generally poor (Aberystwyth Policy Group, 1990). Motorways, dual carriageways and Inter-City train services are generally confined to the north and south coastal regions.

Wales has traditionally lacked a large middle-class, and even today the occupational class profile is clearly different to many parts of England. Wales has an older and ageing population, with a high proportion of retired, early retired and long-term sick (Gorard, 1997a). Social disadvantage is growing in Wales compared to England, with relatively high unemployment, coupled with generally lower levels of economic activity. For example, of the 459 local authority districts in Britain, nine of the 10 with the lowest activity rates for men, and seven of the 10 with the lowest activity rates for women, are in Wales (Istance & Rees, 1995). Weekly wages, for those in work, are among the lowest in the United Kingdom (UK), and this position may be worsened by a trend towards insecure employment, particularly affecting the most vulnerable. On the other hand, there are areas such as Bridgend showing signs of economic retrenchment, and others such as Cardiff showing signs of positive boom.

Wales is officially a bilingual nation, and all major organisations have a Welsh Language policy (including the media). This is a protective measure because only a minority of the population speak Welsh, and even those who speak Welsh also speak English. In general, the less-developed and northern rural parts of Wales have a majority of Welsh-speakers, while the eastern counties and coastal cities have a majority of English monoglots. Confusingly, the majority of Welsh-speakers live in the more densely populated and predominantly English-speaking areas, such as Cardiff. In general, the Welsh-speakers are of higher educational and occupational status than their English-speaking counterparts. For example, although the Census suggested a figure of around 8% of the population of South Wales able to speak some Welsh, only around 1% actually speak Welsh at home (Gorard et al, 1997), and these are over-represented in the highest social classes in South Wales (Giggs & Pattie, 1994).

*Educational Differences*

Despite earlier attitudes stemming from a 'for Wales, see England' mentality, the education system in Wales is now markedly different to that in England, more so than simple regional variations within England, and the differences are increasing (e.g. Raffe et al, 1997). Initial education in Wales is administered by the Welsh Office (now the administration for the National Assembly), not the Department for Education and Employment. The majority of public examinations are taken using papers from the Welsh Joint Education Committee. There are several differences between the National Curriculum for Wales, and that for England, with subjects such as History, Geography, Art and Music having separate orders. The differences are in perspective as well as content, since, according to legislation, all pupils in Wales have the right to learn about Welsh language, culture and history. There is, or should be, a 'general Welshness pervading pupil's learning experiences' (Jones & Lewis, 1995, p. 24). The National Curriculum for

Wales also specifies that Welsh language teaching is compulsory in all state-funded schools. This extra subject, simply grafted on to the existing National Curriculum for Wales, is a key issue for education in Wales with political, resource, equal opportunities and standards implications.

Low population density and travel restrictions mean that many families in rural areas effectively have no choice of schools. Early reports suggest that active choice, or deselection of the local school, is consequently much higher in urban areas than rural (Adler et al, 1989), and in areas where there are more schools (Echols et al, 1990). Some rural areas are in fact still running a pure catchment area system, allocating places by proximity where a school is over-subscribed (Hammond & Dennison, 1995; White et al, 1999). The remoteness of parts of Wales mean that schools are either smaller than in England with fewer facilities and more limited curricula, or children have to travel further there and back each day. In selecting a school, families, particularly those from rural areas, face a choice from limited options of little diversity. Reynolds (1990) has claimed that 40% of parents in Wales had no choice of secondary school, unless they were prepared to travel 40 or more miles. This estimate is clearly too high, but the point is nevertheless a good one.

The uniformity of schools in Wales is remarkable. Among the 2,048 schools of all types in Wales in 1994, there were no City Technology Colleges, or similarly specialist schools for drama, sport, or languages. There were only 15 Grant Maintained (GM) schools altogether. In fact, fewer than 1% of schools in Wales opted out, compared to more than 4% in England (Halpin et al 1997), and even the larger number of GM (as they then were) schools in England has not produced much diversity of provision, since many seem to be reviving an academic model based upon tradition and selectivity (Fitz et al, 1995). Of the 484,322 full-time pupil equivalents in Wales in 1994, only 5% of the school population were in GM, independent, and special schools combined. Parents in Wales do not have a realistic option of using local fee-paying schools, since there are so few such schools, including none in Mid-Wales, and only eight which until recently were able to offer Assisted Places. The established market of the fee-paying sector in Wales is small (1.8%) and diminishing from a peak in 1960. In England, 7.9% of pupils attend independent schools, making the sector four times larger than in Wales (and growing). On the other hand, Wales has one type of school unknown in England, the *Ysgolion Cymraeg* or Welsh-medium schools which are, in theory at least, non-selective and of equal prestige to the other LEA-controlled comprehensives. In fact, they have very impressive pupil outcomes and in a market-like situation are therefore being used by non-Welsh speaking families, leading to an increase in their size and number.

One outcome of the increasing separation of Welsh educational policy from that of England (Delamont & Rees, 1997) has been the development of school 'improvement' measures and attainment targets specific to Wales, prompted to a large extent by the view that schools in Wales are generally not performing as well as schools in England. It has been shown elsewhere how the notion that schools in England are outperforming those in Wales is seductive (Gorard, 1998a). The Wales 'effect' has been used by school-effectiveness researchers to demonstrate the importance of what happens in schools in determining results (Reynolds, 1995), and by politicians as a spur for regional school-improvement. It is generally based upon raw-score comparisons (Jones, 1996), or raw-score comparisons with some attempt to argue a match between the comparison groups (Reynolds, 1990). This prevailing view is reinforced by memories of the high 'failure rate' in Wales after 1944 (in Istance and Rees, 1995), the findings of the 1981 Loosemore Report, more recent inspection reports (Office of Her Majesty's Chief Inspector for Wales, 1993), the relatively low level of qualification among the working population in Wales (Eurostat, 1995), and by the publication of 'league tables' of school examination results (*The Times Educational Supplement*, 1995). On almost any score of educational achievement that can be devised, it seems that the results in Wales are inferior to those in England, and these comparisons have had real implications for local educational policies. For example, this negative view of the effectiveness of schools in Wales was taken up by policy-makers in the previous government who made it the cornerstone of their improvement strategy and targets (Welsh Office, 1995a,b, 1996, 1997a). This approach has been continued by the new administration, underlying the important message of the White Paper put before parliament called *Building Excellent Schools Together* which states that 'standards of achievement are still far too low, progress in raising them far too slow ...' (Welsh Office, 1997b, p. 2 in summary). This is justified by statements such as, 'results at GCSE A*-C lag behind those in England .... 11% of pupils leave school without GCSEs, where 8% do so in England' (p. 3).

These and other differences may have led to an increasing separation of Welsh educational policy from that of England. However, they have not yet led to a separate and distinctive 'policy sociology' for Wales (Delamont & Rees, 1997), where one observer described education policy research as still in its infancy (Phillips, 1996). Policy-making in Wales has been characterised as the 'mediation' by the Welsh Office, and pressure groups, of policy imperatives whose origin is in England.[1] The new National Assembly may lead to further separation of the educational policies of England and Wales, with the Assembly responsible for the allocation of the educational budget. Nevertheless, the scale of the changes may be small since national legislation such as the Education Reform Act 1988 will still be in force, the amount of the budget will be decided in Westminster, and much of the money is anyway already committed to existing institutions. It should also be recalled that the referendum result in favour of the Assembly was not only of the narrowest margin, it was regionally divided. In the opinion of some commentators this should force the Assembly to respect regional differences within Wales.

### Research Findings from Wales

The first thing to note is that until very recently there has been a relative paucity of educational policy research specific to Wales, presumably stemming from the 'England *and* Wales' history. The new growing body of educational research in Wales has produced several surprises in the form of findings that have not only disagreed with equivalent studies in England, but have identified opposite processes at work. Some of these may be explicable in terms of the structural differences between the two regions (but see below).

*Choice*

The example of school choice is already reasonably well-known. The low population density in Wales means that the process of parental choice is very different from the London LEAs used by many studies. Perhaps the simplest difference concerns reports about the number of schools considered by families when making a choice – their choice set. Choice sets of five to seven schools have been described in England, and in their book on markets, Gewirtz et al (1995) illustrate their ideal type of 'disconnected' parents, who do not engage with the market at all, as deciding to look at only *two* schools (and by implication this woman is aware of a greater range of options). A recent study in South Wales found that the average size of the choice set was less than two schools, even for the most privileged families (Gorard, 1997b).

Another key difference could be in the choice criteria emerging from different studies. Academic outcomes, proximity, and pupil selection have all emerged as themes in the accounts from research in England, but in Wales schools are reportedly chosen on completely different grounds (Table I). Families were presented with an outline of 73 potential reasons for selecting a new school and asked to rate the importance of each to the choice that they had made/were making. In summary, although various criteria may be found to be more significant to some groups of respondents than others, families are chiefly concerned with child security rather than outcomes, while preferring tolerance and a pleasant ethos to selection, and convenience. None of the variables rated as very important in this study can be classed as situational, organisational, or selective criteria (see Gorard, 1997b). In not finding an important role for situational criteria, such as travel, this study is very much in a minority (cf. West et al, 1995). These low ratings for situational criteria are even more interesting, since the results of this study are unusual in including the views of children who are thought to be more concerned with such practical issues. Intriguingly, travel was rated as less important by families in rural areas than those in urban areas, and correspondingly rated as more significant to those considering a larger choice set.

More surprising is the absence of direct evidence of a strong desire for any kind of pupil selection. Single-sex, religion, ability, and social class are all missing as significant influences on school choice. It could be argued that variables such as *well-behaved pupils* actually represent a type of unconscious code for class or social background, or that a desire for good *examination results* from a school is actually a desire for high-ability pupils in an era of raw-score performance indicators, but there are two arguments against this. First, such variables are linked by multivariate analysis with others, that have no such underlying selective message. The school's facilities, for example, are strongly linked by principal components analysis to examination results, but do not appear to imply any kind of pupil selection at all. Secondly, several other variables, not rated as nearly as important overall, explicitly measure views on selection, including *clever pupils*; *nice pupils*; *single-sex*; *middle-class pupils*; *religion*; *ethnic mix*, *Welsh ethos* and the *proportion of British pupils*. It could also be countered that families want selection, but are not willing to state it openly, as was suggested by the findings of Bagley (1995), but this view is both unparsimonious, and unsupported by the frank and unembarassed comments of many respondents on their forms, and later in the interviews.

| Criterion | Mean (max 2.00) | Standard deviation | Number of cases |
|---|---|---|---|
| Happiness | 1.84 | .40 | 1029 |
| Good teaching | 1.77 | .51 | 1248 |
| No bullying | 1.76 | .53 | 1207 |
| Pupil safety | 1.75 | .49 | 1070 |
| Teacher qualification | 1.73 | .51 | 1026 |
| Work atmosphere | 1.72 | .51 | 1206 |
| Teaches respect | 1.71 | .51 | 1076 |
| Caring staff | 1.71 | .53 | 1201 |
| Well-managed | 1.71 | 0.52 | 1073 |

Table I. Most important criteria in school choice.

## The Social Impact of Markets

There is very little evidence so far of the educational outcomes of the market reforms in either England or Wales. In terms of social segregation between schools, the majority of evidence from England is that the process of choice is further advantaging already privileged families, leading to the commonly accepted notion that segregation between schools is therefore increasing. The near-consensus from research on the process of school choice in England appears to be that the limited market is a class strategy used to extend the privilege of the already privileged (see for example Ball et al, 1996; Conway, 1997; Reay, 1998; Whitty et al, 1998).

A recent analysis of the situation in South Wales on the other hand suggests that social segregation is, and has been, decreasing from a stratification index of 24% in 1991/92 to 21% in 1996/97 (Gorard & Fitz, 1998a). The method of analysis was a relatively simple one that can be used at any level of aggregation, and for any combination of schools. The segregation between schools, in any unit of analysis such as a Local Education Authority, is defined as the proportion of its students who would have to change schools for there to be an even spread of disadvantage between schools (i.e. for the number of students eligible for free school meals in each LEA to be distributed between schools in proportion to their number on roll). More precisely the segregation index is:

$$SUM(|\text{free meals in schools} - (\text{free meals in LEA} * \text{students in school/students in LEA})|)$$
$$/ 2*\text{free meals in LEA}.$$

Once this calculation has been understood it can be seen to be precisely what is meant by the term 'segregation' in this context. It can be used to decide whether schools are becoming more or less mixed in terms of parental income, or any other indicator of social disadvantage, such as ethnicity, stages of English, or special needs (which can be substituted for eligibility for free school meals). The results for Swansea LEA are shown in Figure 1. Despite a growth in the number of placement requests and huge growth in the number of appeals, the market in South Wales does not seem to lead to the increased stratification that some critics fear.

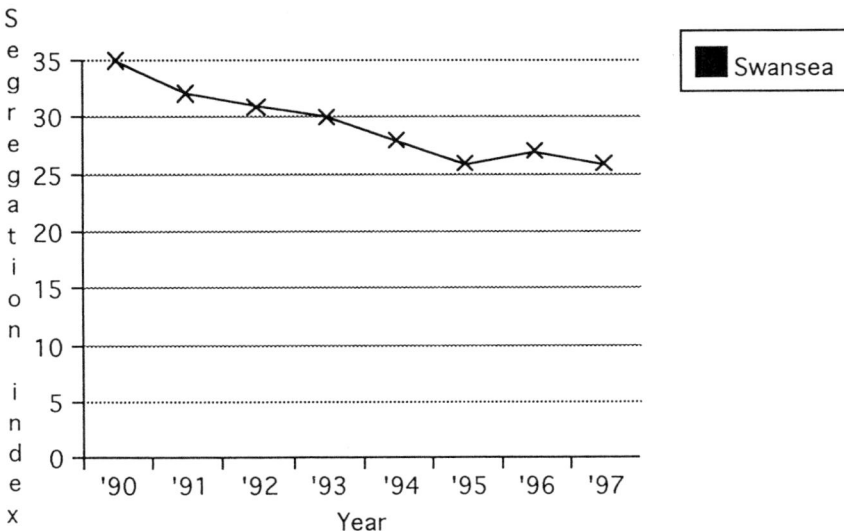

Figure 1. Changes in segregation between school over time (Swansea).

The LEAs' declared policy of matched (feeder) primary schools and the standard-number limitation built into existing legislation may have constrained any greater drive towards reduced stratification. The number of pupils from outside the catchment area of the matched primaries accepted at each of the 'popular' secondary schools is so low that the effect of the market has been muted. Competition for these few places is now so fierce that it might appear it would be predominantly the most privileged members of society who would win the ensuing struggle. In fact, there is evidence of the reverse in South Wales. The most popular schools in Cardiff, Swansea and Rhondda Cynon Taff, while still taking fewer pupils eligible for free school meals than their 'ideal' fair share, have moved consistently towards the ideal since the Education Reform Act 1988. Popular schools then are increasing their proportion of children from economically disadvantaged families. Archetypal among these schools are the relatively newly designated *Ysgolion Cymraeg* which started from a small relatively privileged base of predominantly Welsh-speaking families, and have grown in both size and disadvantage ratio over the period of study.

### Gender

While studies from England have suggested that the difference between the comparative performance of boys and girls is increasing (Stobart et al, 1992; Arnot et al, 1996), and that the apparent under-achievement of boys is concentrated at the lower end of attainment (*The Observer*, 1998; *The Times Educational Supplement*, 1998), a recent study from Wales has found almost exactly the opposite trends (Gorard et al, 1999). The data used in this study are the Key Stage statutory assessment and GCSE examination results for all pupils at school in Wales from 1992 to 1997. The analysis focuses on the gap in achievement between boys and girls (the 'achievement gap') at each age for each grade or level and subject. The achievement gap has been calculated at each grade level for each subject individually, for each year, for all of Wales; and for all subjects combined, at each grade level, for each year, for all of Wales. Accordingly, this study provides a much more detailed analysis of patterns of relative performance, and using higher quality data on the age cohort, than most previous studies have done, not only in Wales, but also elsewhere in the UK.

Calculation of the achievement gap requires a preliminary analysis of the patterns of entry for boys and girls in each subject, which give rise to an 'entry gap'. The entry gap for an assessment is defined as the difference between the entries for girls and boys relative to the relevant age cohort for Key Stage 1 to Key Stage 3; and relative to the entries from the age cohort for GCSE. The result is the difference between the percentage of the entry for any assessment who are girls and the percentage of the entry for any assessment who are boys. The *entry gap* for an assessment is defined as the difference between the entries for girls and boys relative to the relevant age cohort for Key Stage 1 to Key Stage 3; and relative to the entries from the age cohort for GCSE.

$$Entry\ Gap = (GE-BE)/(GE+BE).100$$

where GE = number of girls entered (or in the age cohort); and BE = number of boys entered (or in the age cohort)

For example, if 700 girls and 300 boys enter English A Level, the entry gap would be 40%.

The achievement gap for each grade within an assessment such as GCSE is defined as the difference between the performances of boys and girls, relative to the performance of all entries, minus the entry gap. The achievement gap is thus a measure of the relative achievement of each gender for any grade level. The *achievement gap* for each grade within an assessment is defined as the difference between the performances of boys and girls, relative to the performance of all entries, minus the entry gap.

$$Achievement\ Gap = (GP-BP)/(GP+BP).100 - Entry\ Gap$$

where GP = the number of girls achieving that grade or better; BP = the number of boys achieving that grade or better.

For example, if 500 girls and 500 boys enter Italian GCSE, while 300 girls and 200 boys get graded C or above, then the achievement gap at grade C or above is: (300–200)/(300+200).100–0 = 20% (since the entry gap is zero and where a positive value is in favour of girls). To put this in plainer terms, 50% of the candidates attained a C or above. If there was no gender gap, we would expect 250 girls to attain a C or above. In fact 300 did, or 20% more than we expect. Similarly we expect a figure of 250 for boys, and the actual 200 is 20% below what we expect. Therefore the achievement gap is 20%.

| Year/Grade | A | C | G |
|---|---|---|---|
| 1992 | 14 | 7 | 0 |
| 1993 | 18 | 7 | 0 |
| 1994 | 15 | 8 | 1 |
| 1995 | 18 | 8 | 1 |
| 1996 | 19 | 8 | 1 |
| 1997 | 19 | 8 | 0 |

Table II. Achievement gap in favour of girls: all GCSE subjects.

When all subject entries are combined for analysis, there is no achievement gap at the lowest possible grade (level 1) at any Key Stage. The gaps appear, always in favour of girls, at level 2 in Key Stage 1 (5% in 1996). The achievement gaps increase geometrically with every grade level, reaching up to 10% at level 7 in Key Stage 3. There is no indication that these gaps are increasing over time. At GCSE there is a continuing overall achievement gap in favour of girls (see Table II). This gap is not apparent at the lowest possible level of those who achieve a grade G or above, but, as with Key Stage 1 to Key Stage 3, it increases in a clear progression with every grade level above G (see for example Figure 2 which shows the gap at A* rising to 24%). The introduction of the A* grade in 1994 has served to increase the differential between boys and girls at the highest level.

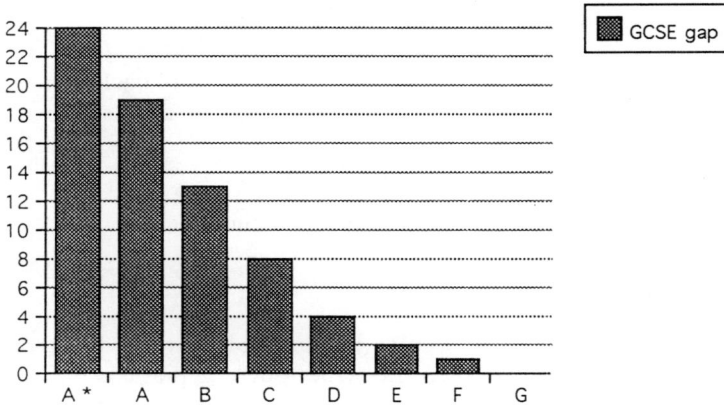

Figure 2. Achievement gaps in favour of girls in 1997: all GCSE subjects.

As Table III shows, the gap between boys and girls in terms of aggregate measures of achievement has declined in Wales since 1992. This is true of attainment at lower levels of achievement such as grade G or above at GCSE for example, as well as for the more usually cited 'benchmark' of 5 or more GCSEs at grades A*-C. The equivalent gap at grades A*-G has dropped from 12% in favour of girls in 1992 to 7% in favour of girls in 1997. As with individual subject entries therefore, the gender achievement gap is more of a problem at high levels of achievement.

| Year | Boys | Girls | Point difference | Achievement gap |
|------|------|-------|------------------|-----------------|
| 1992 | 28 | 38 | 10 | 15 |
| 1997 | 39 | 49 | 10 | 11 |

Table III. Percentage gaining five GCSEs at grade C or above in Wales.

### For England, See Wales

Although there is insufficient space here to examine all the apparent differences in findings from Wales and England in detail, and although some of the educational differences are predictable from the general differences between the two areas, it is suggested that others can be resolved by consideration of the methods used. In summary, educational processes in Wales and England may be more similar than they are different (there may be larger differences within England), and the smaller scale of the nation-state of Wales may give social scientists a more convenient social laboratory in which to carry out their research.

First, in terms of outcome measures, there are no clear differences between the effectiveness of schools in Wales and schools in England once allowance is made for variations in the socio-economic background of the intake (Gorard, 1998a,b). Second, although there have been suggestions that the idiosyncratic process of choice in Wales is determined chiefly by the nature of schooling there, at least some of the differences may be due to methodological problems, especially omitted variable bias in prior studies (Gorard, 1997c, 1998c). Most importantly, for the purposes of this chapter, the little secondary analysis of data from England that has been possible suggests that trends in between-school segregation and the apparent under-achievement of boys are the same in England as they were first found to be in Wales.

One interpretation of the findings in Wales with regard to between-school segregation is that whatever the stratifying effects of market forces and competition may be, the effects of catchment areas or zoning and 'selection by mortgage' may have been a good deal worse. What some commentators appear to assume is that the situation was somehow *less* stratified before 1988 in England and Wales. One would only expect the introduction of schemes of choice to lead to segregation if they started from a relatively well-integrated system. They did not (Hirsch, 1997). The picture presented in Figure 1 though, indicates a considerable degree of social segregation before the impact of policies of parental choice. In other words, prior to 1988 in England and Wales, local patterns of use and preference already led to clear segregation by income and social class (the figures for Oxfordshire from 1989 to 1997 are 38, 36, 35, 32, 31, 30, 31, 29, 29). When policies of choice and competition were superimposed on this pattern of use, there was often a noticeable, but temporary, increase in the segregation index for a year or two. The figures for Lambeth and Wandsworth in London are used here as typical examples (Figure 3). Segregation then declines and settles at a lower level than before, as the market becomes 'established'. If some sections of society are more aware of changes in policy and more attuned to their new rights as 'consumers', one might expect that these 'alert clients' would produce a shift towards stratification in the immediate aftermath of choice reforms whatever the long-term outcomes. This is what is termed here the 'starting-gun effect'.

Although more privileged families may, at the outset, be more alert to their new rights under choice legislation, and more capable of making a choice in the short term, in the longer term choice may become more popular (Echols et al, 1990) with the poorer sections of any community eventually participating fully (Cookson, 1994). That this is so is evidenced by DfEE data on the growth of appeals, and the indication that this growth is set to continue, and taking into consideration the fact that appeals are only relevant to those not obtaining their first choice of school, it can be deduced that the proportion of alert clients has grown significantly since 1988. Those studies made immediately after the introduction of policies to increase school choice, such as the Education Reform Act 1988, may quite validly produce quite different findings from those of studies made some time later. The concept of the established market can help reconcile the findings of the two (Gorard & Fitz, 1998b).

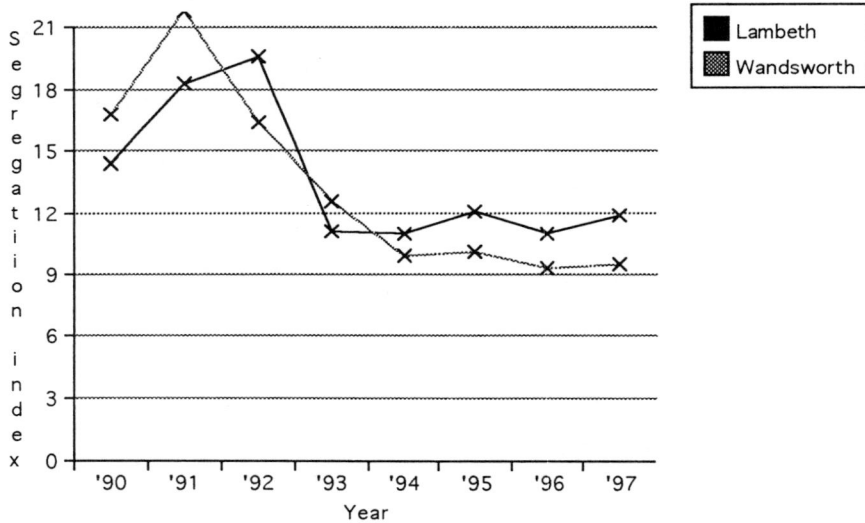

Figure 3. Changes in segregation between school over time (London).

| Year | Boys | Girls | Point difference | Achievement gap |
|------|------|-------|------------------|-----------------|
| 1992 | 34 | 43 | 9 | 12 |
| 1997 | 40 | 49 | 9 | 10 |

Table IV. Percentage gaining five GCSEs at grade C or above in England.

A similar conclusion may be reached concerning the comparative performance of boys and girls at school in Wales and England. Again, methodological differences are more likely than regional variations to account for the disparate research results (Gorard, 1999). For example, if the aggregate GCSE results in England are calculated in the same way as in Wales, the apparent gap between boys and girls is also declining (Table IV).

In each example, it may be more a case of – 'for England, see Wales'. There are also implications for the conduct of educational research, as discussed by Gorard (1998d) and picked up by Hillage et al (1998), but these will have to remain the subject of another paper.

## Note

[1] A previous Permanent Secretary is alleged to have recorded that when a memo from Whitehall arrives at the Scottish Office, the reponses is 'how can we use this to benefit Scotland?'. When a memo arrives at the Welsh Office, the response is 'what do you think Whitehall wants us to do?'.

## References

Aberystwyth Policy Group (1990) *Secondary Education in Rural Wales*. Aberystwyth: Faculty of Education, University of Wales.

Adler, M., Petch, A. & Tweedie, J. (1989) *Parental Choice and Educational Policy*. Edinburgh: Edinburgh University Press.

Arnot, M., David, M. & Weiner, G. (1996) *Educational Reform and Gender Equality in Schools*. Manchester: Equal Opportunities Commission.

Bagley, C. (1995) Black and White Unite or Flight? The racial dimension of schooling and parental choice, paper presented to the British Educational Research Association Annual Conference, September, Bath.

Ball, S., Bowe, R. & Gewirtz, S. (1996) School Choice, Social Class and Distinction: the realization of advantage in education, *Journal of Education Policy*, 11, pp. 89–112.

Conway, S. (1997) The Reproduction of Exclusion and Disadvantage: symbolic violence and social class inequalities in 'parental choice' of secondary education, *Sociological Research On-line*, 2(4).

Cookson, P. (1994) *School Choice*. London: Yale University Press.

Delamont, S. & Rees, G. (1997) *Understanding the Welsh Education System: does Wales need a separate 'policy sociology'? Working Paper 23*. Cardiff: School of Education.

Echols, F., McPherson, A. & Willms, J. (1990) Parental Choice in Scotland, *Journal of Educational Policy*, 5, pp. 207–222.

Eurostat (1995) *Education across the European Union – statistics and indicators*. Brussels: Statistical Office of the European Communities.

Fitz, J., Halpin, D. & Power, S. (1995) Opting into the Past? Grant Maintained Schools and the Reinvention of Tradition, paper presented at ESRC/CEPAM Invitation Seminar, February, Milton Keynes.

Gewirtz, S., Ball, S. & Bowe, R. (1995) *Markets, Choice and Equity in Education*. Buckingham: Open University Press.

Giggs, J. & Pattie, C. (1994) Wales as a Plural Society, *Contemporary Wales*, 5, p. 25

Gorard, S. (1997a) *The Region of Study: patterns of participation in adult education and training. Working paper 1.* Cardiff: School of Education.

Gorard, S. (1997b) *School Choice in an Established Market.* Aldershot: Ashgate.

Gorard, S. (1997c) A Choice of Methods: the methodology of choice, *Research in Education*, 57, pp. 45–56.

Gorard, S. (1998a) Schooled to Fail? Revisiting the Welsh School-effect, *Journal of Education Policy*, 13, pp. 115–124.

Gorard, S. (1998b) In Defence of Local Comprehensive Schools in South Wales, *Forum*, 40, pp. 58–59.

Gorard, S. (1998c) Social Movement in Undeveloped Markets: an apparent contradiction, *Educational Review*, 50, pp. 249–258.

Gorard, S. (1998d) The Middle Way, British Educational Research Association (BERA) Internet Conference April, www.scre.ac.uk/bera /debate/index.html

Gorard, S. (1999) Keeping a Sense of Proportion: the 'politician's error' in analysing school outcomes, *British Journal of Educational Studies*, 47, pp. 235–246.

Gorard, S., Fevre, R., Rees, G. & Furlong, J. (1997) *Space, Mobility and the Education of Minority Groups in Wales: the survey results, patterns of participation in adult education and training. Working Paper 10.* Cardiff: School of Education.

Gorard, S. & Fitz, J. (1998a) The More Things Change ... The Missing Impact of Marketisation, *British Journal of Sociology of Education*, 19, pp. 365–376

Gorard, S. & Fitz, J. (1998b) Under Starters Orders: the established market, the Cardiff study and the Smithfield project, *International Studies in Sociology of Education*, 8, pp. 299–314.

Gorard, S., Salisbury, J., Rees, G. & Fitz, J. (1999) *The Comparative Performance of Boys and Girls at School in Wales*, report commissioned by Qualification, Curriculum and Assessment Authority for Wales (ACCAC). Cardiff: ACCAC.

Halpin, D., Power, S. & Fitz, J. (1997) Opting into the Past? Grant Maintained Schools and the Reinvention of Tradition, in R. Glatter, P. Woods & C. Bagley (Eds) *Choice and Diversity in Schooling. Perspectives and Prospects.* London: Routledge.

Hammond, T. & Dennison, W. (1995) School Choice in Less Populated Areas, *Educational Management and Administration*, 23, pp. 104–113.

Hillage, J., Pearson, R., Anderson, A. & Tomkin, P. (1998) *Excellence in Research in Schools.* Sudbury: DfEE Publications.

Hirsch, D. (1997) What Can Britain Learn from Abroad?, in R. Glatter, P. Woods, & C. Bagley (Eds) *Choice and Diversity in Schooling. Perspectives and Prospects.* London: Routledge.

Istance, D. & Rees, G. (1995) *Lifelong Learning in Wales: a programme for prosperity*, a NIACE Cymru policy discussion paper. Leicester: NIACE.

Jones, G. (1996) *Wales 2010 Three Years On.* Cardiff: Institute of Welsh Affairs.

Jones, B. & Lewis, I. (1995) A Curriculum Cymreig, *The Welsh Journal of Education*, 4(2), pp. 22–35.

*Observer [The]* (1998) The Trouble with Boys, 4 January, p. 13.

Office of Her Majesty's Chief Inspector for Wales (1993) *Achievement and Under-achievement in Secondary Schools in Wales, 1991–92*, Occasional Paper 1. Cardiff: Office of Her Majesty's Chief Inspector for Wales.

Phillips, R. (1996) Education Policy Making in Wales: a research agenda, *Welsh Journal of Education*, 5(2), pp. 26–42.

Raffe, D., Brannen, K., Croxford, L. & Martin, C. (1997) The Case for 'Home Internationals' in Comparative Research: comparing England, Scotland, Wales and Northern Ireland, paper presented to European Research Network on Transitions in Youth, Annual Workshop, Dublin.

Reay, D. (1998) Engendering Social Reproduction: mothers in the educational marketplace, *British Journal of Sociology of Education*, 19, pp. 195–209.

Reynolds, D. (1990) The Great Welsh Education Debate, *History of Education*, 19, pp. 251–257.

Reynolds, D. (1995) Creating an Educational System for Wales, *The Welsh Journal of Education*, 4(2), pp. 4–21.

Stobart, G., Elwood, J. & Quinlan, M. (1992) Gender Bias in Examinations: how equal are the opportunities?, *British Educational Research Journal*, 18, pp. 261–76.

*The Times Educational Supplement* (1995) The Times Educational Supplement School and College Performance Tables 1995.

*The Times Educational Supplement* (1998) Poverty Gap Beats Gender Divide, 16 January, p. 23.

Welsh Office (1995a) *A Bright Future: getting the best for every pupil at school in Wales*. Cardiff: Her Majesty's Stationery Office (HMSO).

Welsh Office (1995b) *A Bright Future: the way forward*. Cardiff: HMSO.

Welsh Office (1995c) *Statistics of Education and Training in Wales: Schools No. 3*. Cardiff: HMSO.

Welsh Office (1996) *A Bright Future: statistical update*. Cardiff: HMSO.

Welsh Office (1997a) *A Bright Future: beating the previous best*. Cardiff: HMSO.

Welsh Office (1997b) *Building Excellent Schools Together*. Cardiff: HMSO.

West, A., David, M., Hailes, J. & Ribbens, J. (1995) Parents and the Process of Choosing Secondary Schools: implications for schools, *Educational Management and Administration*, 23, pp. 28–38.

White, P., Gorard, S. & Fitz, J. (1999) *An Analysis of Local School Admission Arrangements*. Cardiff: School of Social Sciences.

Whitty, G., Power, S. & Halpin, D. (1998) *Devolution and Choice in Education*. Buckingham: Open University Press.

# Unifying Academic and Vocational Learning: current policy developments in Wales

## DAVID RAFFE, KEN SPOURS, MICHAEL YOUNG & CATHY HOWIESON

### Introduction

The three home countries (England, Scotland and Wales) of Great Britain are pursuing different if not divergent strategies for post-16 education and training. Their post-compulsory education systems face similar problems and challenges, many of which are also faced by other European countries; like most other European countries their response is to develop closer links between academic and vocational learning and to reduce the divisions between curricular tracks (Lasonen & Young, 1998; Raffe & Lasonen, 1998). All three countries are moving in the direction of 'unification' of academic and vocational learning, but their strategies for unification differ significantly. In England current policies exemplify a 'linkages' strategy which maintains the three main tracks but emphasises their similarity and equivalence and develops closer links between them. In Scotland current reforms are bringing the tracks together into a single unified system (Howieson et al, 1997). In this chapter we examine policy developments in Wales, and address two related questions: what scope is there for Wales to develop a policy that is distinctive from England, and how does the Welsh approach compare with the linkages and unified system strategies adopted in England and Scotland respectively?

This chapter is a product of the ESRC-funded Unified Learning Project, which has compared approaches to unifying academic and vocational learning in Scotland, England and Wales. We begin with a brief summary of the conceptual framework which we developed within the project in order to analyse these approaches. We then consider the various barriers to Wales adopting a more 'unified' strategy. Finally we examine three current developments in Wales which may be seen as ways of overcoming these barriers. At the time of writing, in 1998, the specific outcomes of these developments are not easy to predict. However, we conclude that through these developments and other current changes, in particular the establishment in 1999 of the National Assembly for Wales, a distinctive policy on unifying academic and vocational learning in Wales could emerge.

## Issues in the Unification of Academic and Vocational Learning

Between 1996 and 1998 the Unified Learning Project compared English and Scottish developments in post-16 education and studied issues which have arisen from the strategies adopted in the two countries. The Project developed a conceptual framework for analysing the unification of academic and vocational learning in post-compulsory education and training systems (Young et al, 1997; Raffe et al, 1998). The conceptual framework is based on a distinction between three types of system: a tracked system, with separate and distinctive tracks; a linked system, with features linking the tracks or common properties which underline their similarity or equivalence; and a unified system, which does not use tracks to organise provision and accommodates a diversity of provision within a unified set of arrangements. These three types can be seen as points along a continuum of 'unification', with tracked systems at one end, various forms of linked systems in the middle, and unified systems at the other end. The continuum can apply to different dimensions of unification such as curriculum, assessment, certification and institutions. Systems may vary in their profile across the different dimensions; for example a system could have tracked qualifications delivered through a unified system of tertiary institutions.

We also identify three policy strategies corresponding to the three types of system: respectively, track-based, linkages and unified system strategies. Each seeks either to develop or to consolidate features of the corresponding type of system. The general trend of policy in most European countries is to move in the direction of a unified system, away from tracking towards either a linked or unified system. We refer to these as 'strategies for unification'.

We have applied this framework to the post-compulsory education and training systems of England and Scotland and argue that on balance, England is an example of a tracked system, and Scotland of a linked system, although both systems vary across the different dimensions of unification. In each country current policies aim to move the system in the direction of unification. In England Sir Ron Dearing's (1996) *Review of Qualifications for 16–19 Year Olds*, the ensuing *Qualifying for Success* consultation (Department for Education and Employment [DfEE], 1997) launched by the new Labour government, and the government's response to that consultation (DfEE, 1998a) all exemplify a 'linkages' strategy which maintains the three main tracks but emphasises their similarities and equivalences and seeks closer links between them. (The Dearing Review and the *Qualifying for Success* consultation also covered Wales, as we discuss below.) In other words government policies for England aim to move it from a tracked system to a linked one. In Scotland the Higher Still reform is setting out to bring the tracks together into a single unified system (Scottish Office, 1994).

This policy divergence – or difference – was made possible, even before the establishment of the Scottish Parliament, by the existence of the separate institutions of Scottish education and the relative autonomy in policy-making that they allowed. The decision to adopt a different strategy for Scotland can be attributed to several different factors. First, the small scale and relative uniformity of the Scottish system make a unified system approach more feasible (Raffe et al, 1998a). Second, the educational and political culture of Scotland, with its more widespread and uniform support for the comprehensive principle and its rejection of tracking, favours a unified system (Howieson et al, 1997). Third, the greater flexibility of the existing system makes it easier to move incrementally towards a unified system (Raffe, 1997).

To what extent do the conditions which promote Scottish divergence from the English model also apply to Wales? The distinctiveness of Welsh institutions and the potential that this gives for autonomous policy-making have been increased by the recent devolution of education and training policy responsibilities, and the creation of new bodies at a Welsh level (Delamont & Rees, 1997). The National Assembly for Wales may encourage further policy divergence. Like the Scottish system, the Welsh education system is much smaller and more uniform than that in England. The educational and political culture of Wales also appears to resemble Scotland more than England, in ways which might favour unification. For example, there is stronger support for comprehensive secondary education, more support for modular approaches, and a smaller and less influential independent sector (IWA, 1994; Gorard, 1997; Jones, 1997). Furthermore, Wales has several current developments with 'unifying potential' on which to build, notably the CREDIS (Credit Framework) project, the WelshBac proposals (both discussed below), a distinctive emphasis in work-based provision, for example a strong drive for Modern Apprenticeships in Engineering, and an emerging Welsh Vocational Education and Training (VET) strategy involving the Welsh Development Agency, the four regional economic development Fora, and the 26 Further Education (FE) colleges.

### Can Wales Pursue an Autonomous Strategy for Unifying Academic and Vocational Learning?

Welsh strategies for unification can only differ from those currently pursued in England to the extent that Wales has the capacity to develop separate policies and to make them effective. There are at least four significant constraints on this capacity.

The first constraint is the qualifications system which Wales shares with England and Northern Ireland. Although England and Scotland are pursuing different strategies for unification, both are qualifications-led: in the language of our conceptual framework, the dimension of certification is the main driver of change. Scotland is able to pursue a different strategy for unification because it has a different qualifications system from England; Wales does not. Furthermore, we found a reluctance to allow Welsh qualifications to diverge significantly from those of England, since this could be seen as jeopardising the interests of Welsh students by giving them qualifications which lacked currency in universities or the job market outside Wales. Half of Welsh higher education students attend institutions outside Wales (Rees, 1997). So, while the debates leading up to the current Scottish policies have for the most part been conducted independently of those south of the Border (Howieson et al, 1997), in Wales the current policy debates are framed, at least at governmental level, by the same or similar policy documents as for England. The Dearing Review and the *Qualifying for Success* consultation covered Wales as well as England. An exception, to which we return later in this chapter, is the Welsh Office's (1998) Green Paper *Learning is for Everyone*, which has a distinctively different emphasis from the parallel English Green Paper, *The Learning Age* (DfEE, 1998b).

The second factor is the size of the policy-making machinery. The Welsh Office and other central agencies were too small to make separate policy on all aspects of education and training. Welsh policy-makers have had to 'pick and choose' the areas where they invest their efforts (Raffe, 1998). For the most part they haved worked alongside their English colleagues in the policy process, taking advantage of their privileged position within the process to ensure that Welsh interests are protected. The present apparatus for policy-making offered a sound basis for defending Welsh interests within a policy-making partnership; it may be less adequate as a basis for separate policy-making, even after the establishment of the National Assembly for Wales.

The third factor concerns the different ways that national culture is expressed in Wales and Scotland. Scottish culture is expressed in the national institutions of Church, the Law and Education, which differ from those in England. Welsh culture is underpinned more by the Welsh language and, until recently, much less by such national institutions; furthermore, Welsh language speaking is unevenly spread across the country.

The fourth and least tangible constraint is political. The convention that territorial departments such as the Scottish and Welsh Offices applied general UK policies to the circumstances of their territories did not prevent policy divergence in either Scotland or Wales. Nevertheless, in contrast to Scotland, many members of the Welsh policy community have been reluctant to move away from their position of influence within a close partnership with England (see also Rees, 1997). Pressure for a distinctive approach to education has been less strong, or certainly less effective, than in Scotland, although this may be changing as a result of political devolution. On a broader policy level this reluctance was expressed in the much closer vote on devolution in Wales than in Scotland; in a recent lecture, Kevin Morgan,

Professor of European Regional Planning at the University of Wales, Cardiff, distinguished between the Welsh Wales of the North and West which voted for an Assembly and a more 'British' Wales in the East which voted against.

How limiting are these constraints on Welsh policy-making? This is undoubtedly a period of change as separate policy-making machinery is emerging and new Welsh agencies have been created or hived off from their British or UK parent bodies. The National Assembly for Wales may generate stronger political pressure for policy distinctiveness.

With respect to the constraint of the common qualifications structure, our analysis points to three ways in which Wales might nevertheless develop a distinctive strategy. The first is to pursue reforms along other dimensions of unification than certification: for example through intervening directly in the curriculum, reforming local institutions, or reforming the structure of government and regulation. There has already been a substantial degree of curriculum differentiation at the level of National Curriculum. As well as making provision for teaching the Welsh language, the orders are different in history, geography, art, and music and there are different requirements at Key Stage 4. Another dimension of unification along which reform may proceed independently of qualifications is the organisation and structure of local institutions that provide education and training. We describe current developments below. The second possibility (and not necessarily an alternative) is to reform the qualification system in ways which are consistent with the qualifications structure that is common to both England and Wales. Examples of this approach include unitising the qualifications and establishing a national credit framework, and developing an overarching certificate at 18-plus. The third is to develop separate Welsh qualifications such as the proposed WelshBac (Jenkins et al, 1997). This would mean challenging the belief, mentioned earlier, that a Welsh qualification would lack currency elsewhere. The supporters of the WelshBac point out that the International Baccalaureate (IB), its main inspiration, is widely accepted by universities in the UK and overseas. However the currency of the IB may reflect the high status of some of the schools where it is offered as much as any intrinsic features of the IB itself.

We discuss these three possibilities, and the developments which might support or inhibit them, below.

In conclusion, there appears to be significant potential for a distinctive Welsh strategy for unifying academic and vocational learning, even if much of this potential has not yet been realised, and the Welsh Assembly will further increase this potential. In the rest of this paper our emphasis is as much on the possibilities for future developments in Wales as on the developments which had occurred by 1998.

### Government and Regulation

One of the dimensions of unification in our conceptual framework refers to the extent to which there is a single administrative and regulatory system for academic and vocational learning. In both England and Scotland, education and training responsibilities were brought together in 1995 under the same departments of government: respectively the DfEE and the Scottish Office Education and Industry Department (SOEID). There have also been mergers or alliances of the bodies responsible for awarding academic and vocational qualifications, and of the bodies that accredit and regulate these qualifications. These mergers have led to the creation of the Qualifications and Curriculum Authority (QCA) and the Scottish Qualifications Authority (SQA). In Scotland the merger which established the SQA was substantially driven by the strategy for creating a unified system. In England similar mergers are the result of a wider range of political concerns among which unification has hardly been mentioned. For example the creation of the QCA reflected, amongst other concerns, an anxiety about standards in vocational qualifications. Not surprisingly, it was perceived by some as a take-over of the vocational body, the National Council for Vocational Qualifications (NCVQ), by the academic body (SCAA) rather than as a merger (Spours et al, 1998).

The Welsh Office assumed responsibilities for higher education and training in 1992. The Scottish Office assumed these responsibilities in 1992 and 1994 respectively. However in contrast to Scotland, training and education were in different departments of the Welsh Office; and within the Education Department, schools and FE were in different divisions. This contrast may reflect the fact that the separation of training from economic development has been perceived as a greater issue than its separation from education. Welsh Training and Enterprise Councils (TECs) had a narrower remit and were more focused on training than either English TECs or Scottish Local Enterprise Companies (LECs). The number of TECs in Wales was reduced to four, in line with the new regional economic development Fora. The new 'Economic Powerhouse' brings together the functions of the Welsh Development Agency, the Development Board for Rural Wales and the Land Authority for Wales. These developments invite comparison with Scottish Enterprise, although the Scottish experience suggests that a policy which gives priority to integrating training with economic development will need additional measures to ensure that it is also brought closer to education.

In 1997 ACAC, the Welsh Curriculum and Assessment Authority, took over the functions of the Wales Office of the NCVQ. The new body, ACCAC, parallels the QCA in England, except that the creation of ACCAC was formally the outcome of ACAC taking over the NCVQ Office and not merging. However, the process of unification of the regulatory authorities is less complete in the sense that the QCA retains responsibility for accrediting National Vocational Qualifications (NVQs) in Wales, while sharing responsibility with ACCAC for other aspects of the regulation of NVQs. The large cross-border traffic in qualifications means that ACCAC must work in close co-operation with the QCA and its equivalent in Northern Ireland.

Academic and vocational awarding bodies remain separate in Wales. The Welsh Joint Education Committee (WJEC) is responsible for more than 75% of A Levels and GCSEs taken in Wales. (It also has a wider range of functions, in addition to awarding qualifications, than any English awarding body.) It does not award vocational qualifications, although it acts as agent for NVQs and General National Vocational Qualifications (GNVQs) through a unit of the City and Guilds of London Institute which is housed in the same building.

On paper, the institutions of government and regulation in Wales appear to be somewhat more divided between academic and vocational learning, or between education and training, than elsewhere in Britain. However this may not present a major barrier to future policies for unification. The small scale of government, and the pervasiveness of local networks (Rees, 1997) encourage communication and co-ordination across different policy fields even when these are organised in different departments, divisions or agencies. The governmental machinery is in the process of change and is likely to change further under the Assembly. In 1997 the Welsh Office set up an Education and Training Action Group (ETAG), chaired by the minister of education and with representatives of key organisations and interests, 'to set, and gain support for, the necessary strategic direction' (Welsh Office, 1997, p. 62). ETAG is helping to shape the education and training agenda for the Assembly. It is potentially a force for unification, because its remit covers strategy at a Welsh level across the different sectors of education and training.

No discussion of governance in Wales is complete if it does not mention the country's geographical diversity and the potential importance of policy-making at regional and local level. The four Fora provide a new basis for regional strategy and co-ordination, and these or similar bodies are likely to acquire a more formal role in future. This role may include the planning of post-16 provision and will involve addressing some of the institutional issues to which we now turn.

### Institutions

A further dimension of unification in our conceptual framework concerns the local institutions (schools and colleges) in which education and training are delivered. In a 'pure' version of a tracked system there are different institutions for each track, as in Germany; in a unified system there is either a single type of institution or a variety of institutions each able to offer all types of programmes. Both England and Scotland currently represent an intermediate position that is characteristic of a linked system. As we have noted, in both countries the current reform strategies are certification-led, and in neither are there attempts to 'unify' along the institutional dimension (for example by promoting tertiary colleges). However in both countries the reforms may have knock-on effects as new institutional arrangements are required to deliver the new qualifications and curricula. The reforms in both England and Scotland, with their weak curricular prescription and permissive rules of combination, are relatively 'open' about which of the new curricular possibilities are taken up. As a result individual schools and colleges will have a particularly important role in deciding what curriculum elements to offer, how to package them in programmes and how to guide students' choices. (We discuss the concept of 'openness' in the following section.)

The pattern of institutions for delivering post-compulsory education in Wales is similar to that found in England, though slightly differently distributed. There is only one sixth form college, but several tertiary colleges; most students attend a school or an FE college. In 1997, the FE sector (including tertiary colleges) accounted for 38% of A Level entries and a majority of GNVQs, although schools were relatively quick to introduce their own GNVQ provision. Some commentators perceive the market to be overcrowded, with too many providers and too many small and uneconomic teaching groups. There are some examples of school-college collaboration (for example the Cardiff Collegium in which a college and several neighbouring schools are jointly developing GNVQ provision) but in many areas there is perceived to be waste and duplication, compounded by inconsistent quality control, different funding principles and a lack of strategic overview at local level.

Three factors might encourage further collaboration and/or rationalisation of provision. First, a decline in the unit of funding may squeeze out the more wasteful provision and encourage collaboration, mergers or closures. Two college mergers have already taken place since incorporation, largely as a result of cost pressures; as at summer 1998, a third merger was under consideration.

The second factor could be a rationalisation of funding across post-16 courses. The Further Education Funding Council for Wales (FEFCW) is to be wound-up when the Assembly is established; a move towards a more uniform funding formula for post-compulsory programmes in schools and colleges is one possible outcome.

Third, ETAG has paid particular attention to post-16 provision, including questions of co-operation and collaboration among institutions, and it may recommend increased partnership, rationalisation or other changes in the institutional pattern. It is generally agreed that any such changes would require an enhanced capacity for strategic policy-making at local and regional level.

### Certification and Qualification Frameworks

Earlier we identified the common qualifications structure for England and Wales as a major constraint on Welsh policy autonomy and suggested three ways in which a separate strategy might be pursued: by introducing reforms along other dimensions of unification such as government and regulation and the organisation of local institutions; by reforming qualifications in ways which are consistent with the common qualifications structure; or by developing separate Welsh qualifications. Current policies embrace the first two of these three options. We discussed the first option, reforms of government and regulation, and possible institutional changes, in the previous sections. In this section we discuss the second option, reforms of the qualification system within the current structure, such as unitisation, credit frameworks and overarching certificates.

Our comparison of England, Scotland and other European countries has led us to add a further distinction to our conceptual framework that recognises different strategies for unification. This is the distinction between 'open' and 'grouped' models of unification which is shown (in relation to the dimension of certification) in Figure 1, taken from Howieson et al (1998).

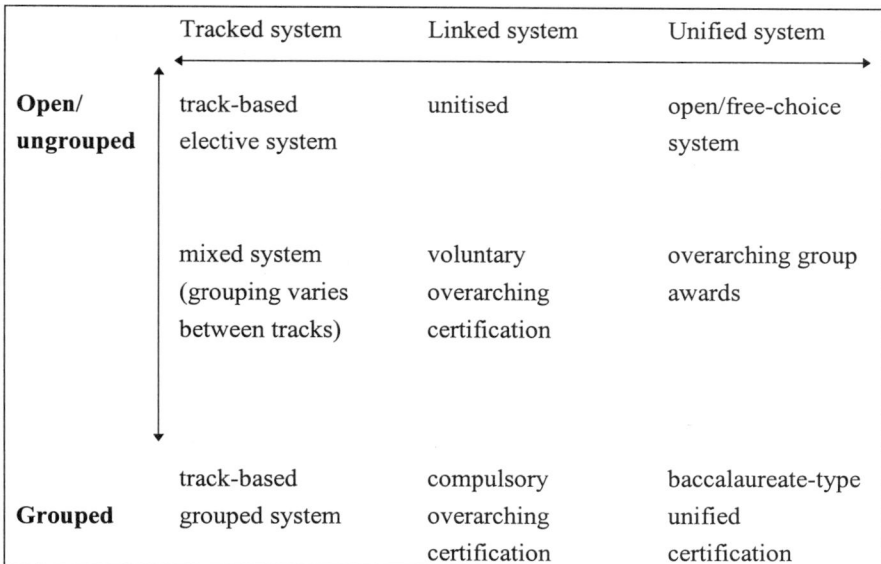

|  | Tracked system | Linked system | Unified system |
|---|---|---|---|
| **Open/ ungrouped** | track-based elective system | unitised | open/free-choice system |
|  | mixed system (grouping varies between tracks) | voluntary overarching certification | overarching group awards |
| **Grouped** | track-based grouped system | compulsory overarching certification | baccalaureate-type unified certification |

Figure 1. Two dimensions of certification: unification and grouping.

Open models tend to be permissive and emphasise flexibility, diversity and choice, while grouped models are more prescriptive and emphasise commonality of experience or entitlement based on overarching curriculum principles such as coherence or breadth. This distinction cuts across many of the dimensions of unification, and it can be applied both to linked and to unified systems. Open linked systems might be based on unitised provision and credit transfer, while grouped linked systems might be based on a compulsory overarching certificate with strong rules of combination that applied across the tracks. The reforms accepted by the government for England following the *Qualifying for Success* consultation represent a partial version of an open model. While emphasising choice and promoting the gradual development of smaller blocks of study (six unit and three unit blocks based on A Levels and GNVQs), the government is cautious about further moves towards an open linked system such as the unitising of all qualifications. It is also cautious about the development of overarching certificates which would take the system towards a grouped model; these are seen as in need of much development work. Among possible models of a unified system, the Scottish Higher Still reform represents a relatively open (or flexible) model: it has flexible entry and exit points and offers free choice from a wide repertoire of modules; group awards will be a voluntary and (probably) minor feature of the system. Higher Still thus stands in contrast to Baccalaureate models of unified system (Finegold et al, 1990; Jenkins et al, 1997) and to the relatively prescriptive unified model based on 'programmes' that has been introduced in Sweden.

Wales has already introduced some of the elements of an open linked system. Between 1993 and 1997 the All Wales Modularisation and Credit Based Development Project developed CREDIS, a post-16 credit framework for education and training below higher education (Fforwm, 1997). CREDIS is managed and owned by Fforwm, the association of Welsh FE colleges, which is responsible for maintaining and updating the central database of units. Fforwm works in association with the Welsh Access Federation, the consortium of the three Open College Networks, which play a critical role in providing quality assurance through peer review. The database now contains 7000 units, which represent more than 90% of college provision, although implementation of the NVQ credit-ratings was delayed pending the outcome of the Beaumont (1996) report. CREDIS is based on the model proposed by the Further Education Unit (FEU) (1992), and divides all qualifications into units of assessment, expressed in terms of level and volume of credit (based on four levels and units of credit equivalent to 30 notional learning hours). A 'Transcript of Student Achievement' records students' achievements of units in terms of credit and level as well as the full qualifications gained. The project distinguishes units (of credit) into which qualifications are divided and modules which are the mechanism through which the college curriculum is delivered. In parallel with the unitisation of credit, the project supported colleges in modularising the delivery of their curriculum.

Any credit framework that is not prescribed by a national agency or department of government depends on substantial central co-ordination and communication and a cross-institutional consensus, especially if a common data base is to be disseminated and regularly updated. These conditions appear to be much easier to satisfy in a relatively small country like Wales, where there are 26 colleges, than in England where there are 450. In England credit systems have only developed in areas such as Leicester where Open College Networks are strong. CREDIS has also benefited from the fact that it operates over the same geographical area as the Welsh Office, and from the government's supportive attitude, although it has always been a bottom-up rather than a top-down project. The Welsh Office's funding of development work that led to CREDIS exemplified a distinctive element in its education policy. In contrast, the DfEE gave little support to the similar proposals that were developed by the FEU in England.

In some ways CREDIS resembles the Action Plan which modularised provision for vocational education in Scotland in 1984 and introduced the National Certificate (Scottish Office Education Department [SED], 1983). However, there are at least three significant differences between CREDIS and the Action Plan. First, the Scottish Action Plan reformed vocational qualifications but left the academic Highers untouched; CREDIS, on the other hand, consists of a unitised and modular structure for all qualifications. Secondly, whereas the Action Plan introduced a wholly new vocational qualification, the National Certificate, CREDIS leaves the qualifications themselves and their assessment systems unchanged. It is not clear, without additional research, whether CREDIS has reduced divisions between academic and vocational learning at the level of the learning experience of students. Thirdly, whereas the Action Plan and the National Certificate were designed primarily for colleges but rapidly spread to schools, CREDIS remains largely based in the college sector. Its semi-official status and its ownership by Fforwm, the independent association of Welsh colleges, may have discouraged the take up of CREDIS by schools. Take-up may also have been inhibited by the greater rigidity of Welsh Sixth Form provision, which, despite the growth of GNVQs, is still dominated by A Levels. This is in contrast to the relatively flexible post-16 curriculum based on Highers that is found in Scottish schools. However the report on the CREDIS development project lists several 'next actions' including 'clear credit-based progression routes established by closer links between schools, FE and HE ...' and 'increased awareness of the CREDIS Unit Database by schools' (Fforwm, 1997, p. 12). The possible implications of moves in the direction of schools are suggested by the decision by the FEFCW to fund GCSEs, A Levels and GNVQs on the basis of credits.

CREDIS is a bottom-up development initiated by the Welsh Further Education Colleges with funding and tacit support from government. In covering 90% of courses offered in the FE sector, it appears to provide two of the necessary conditions – a unitised system of qualifications and a modular curriculum – of a more flexible qualifications framework. However, even though most A Levels and GNVQs that are offered in Welsh colleges are unitised, the different structures of the existing qualifications limit the possibility of credit transfer between them. Furthermore, as CREDIS does not involve any form of overarching certificate that brings together units from different qualifications, it is unlikely, on its own, to encourage 'mixing' across the tracks, except for adult students who are more inclined to take access courses made up of units rather than traditional qualifications.

In its 1998 Green Paper, *Learning is for Everyone*, the Welsh Office announced plans for 'a single national framework: ... an integrated and seamless single qualifications framework post-16'. This will build on CREDIS and the Higher Education Credit Initiative in Wales, and bring all qualifications together into a single system of levels and credits. The Green Paper also suggests that, in the longer term, consideration should be given to whether the framework should be extended to post-14 education. This takes support for a single qualifications framework considerably further than the parallel DfEE Green Paper *The Learning Age* which is far more cautious about the advantages of credits and sees them at best as appropriate only for adults. In responding to the QCA's advice on the *Qualifying for Success* consultation (DfEE, 1998a), the Minister, Baroness Blackstone, was far more sceptical than her opposite number in the Welsh Office about both unitisation and overarching certificates. However even in the Welsh Green Paper there is some ambivalence. While warmly endorsing the idea of a single qualifications framework, at the same time it stresses that:

> *We do not seek to alter the value or the basic characteristics of existing qualifications and awards. (Welsh Office, 1998, p. 26)*

In terms of our conceptual framework, *Learning is for Everyone* appears to be taking Wales further along the continuum towards a unified system than is the case for England, at least on the dimension of certification; it is developing a partially linked open system of qualifications.

### The WelshBac

The third possible response to the constraint of sharing a qualification system with England is to develop separate Welsh qualifications. This is what the WelshBac, first proposed by the Institute of Welsh Affairs (IWA) (1993, 1994), set out to do. An outline proposal for a Welsh Baccalaureate was launched in February 1996 (David & Jenkins, 1996) and the responses to that proposal fed in to a more developed blueprint published in March 1997 (Jenkins et al, 1997). This in turn was the subject of a consultation process, the responses to which are summarised by David & Jenkins (1997).

The most recent (March 1997) proposal for a WelshBac envisages a programme for 16–19-year-olds typically taken over two years. This would include 150 hours of core studies, three 120-hour Standard (S) courses and three 240-hour Higher (H) courses. Breadth would be secured through a requirement that the S and H courses together cover five subject groups, and through the core studies which include such elements as community service, theory of knowledge and global concerns. Six-unit GNVQs at Advanced Level, as proposed by Dearing (1996), could substitute for the corresponding volumes of study on the S and H courses. By implication NVQs or parts of NVQs could be similarly substituted, although this is not spelt out. GNVQs may be used at Foundation, Intermediate or Advanced level and the title of the award would reflect the level of the vocational component.

With its strong emphasis on prescription and breadth the WelshBac stands in contrast to proposals for overarching certificates currently being discussed in England. The IWA envisages that the WelshBac, unlike Dearing's overarching certificate and diploma, would replace A Levels rather than run alongside them. Furthermore, and unlike Higher Still, the WelshBac is designed to over-arch existing vocational qualifications.

The first proposals for the WelshBac (David & Jenkins, 1996) were strongly influenced by the International Baccalaureate, an alternative to A Levels for higher attaining students, which in terms of our framework is a grouped academic qualification within a tracked system. The WelshBac proposal has since been developed into a compulsory overarching certificate to include academic and vocational qualifications within a linked system (see Figure 1). However, in contrast to many unifying reform proposals in England or Scotland, the main target of the WelshBac continues to be the narrowness of the current academic curriculum rather than the inadequacy of provision for middle- or lower-attainers; there are echoes in it of the Higginson Report's proposal for 'five lean A Levels' (Department of Education and Science/Weslsh Office [DES/WO], 1988) as well as the Institute for Public Policy Research proposals for a British Baccalauréat (Finegold et al, 1990). The February 1996 blueprint for the WelshBac (David & Jenkins, 1996) acknowledged the influence of the International Baccalaureate. The March 1997 document (Jenkins et al, 1997) extended the model to over-arch vocational courses and to include different levels of study. The IWA's approach to the WelshBac has thus been to start with a model for academic, high-attaining students and then to extend it down the ability range and widen the scope of its curriculum.

The WelshBac has undoubtedly had a substantial impact on educational debates in Wales. The consultation on the proposals undertaken by the IWA reported positive and often enthusiastic responses from a wide range of interests within the education system and beyond (David and Jenkins, 1997).

However, neither the previous Conservative government nor the Labour government elected in 1997 has supported the WelshBac proposals directly; the latter, though welcoming the proposals as a contribution to debate, turned down a request for funding to support a pilot. Nevertheless the WelshBac has helped to set the terms of the educational debate in which the government is engaged in Wales in a way that has no direct parallels in England. In an article written at the time of the consultation on *Qualifying for*

*Success,* two of the WelshBac's proponents reported that Peter Hain, the Welsh Education Minister, had invited them to consider how its aims might be pursued within the government's framework (Pritchard Jones & David, 1997/98). Later, in his response to the consultation, the Minister asked ACCAC to discuss with the IWA how particular elements of the WelshBac proposals might be pursued within the framework set out in *Qualifying for Success.* The most recent outcome of these discussions is the development of a syllabus framework incorporating the International Baccalaureate and GNVQs.

The WelshBac is an imaginative and ambitious document, and as a blueprint for a qualification for the next century, it is still evolving. It would be most unfair to expect it to have the answers to all possible problems. Comparisons with similar proposals in England (Cramphorn et al, 1997) suggest that, in opting for a 'big bang' approach to qualification reform like the earlier British Baccalaureate, the WelshBac proposals are likely to confront both political and practical difficulties. However, its specific proposals raise a number of issues about how policies on unifying academic and vocational learning in Wales might develop in the next decade and it is to two of these that we now turn.

The first issue concerns progression. The WelshBac is designed as a single programme for 16–19-year-olds; like Scotland's Higher Still it caters for students with different levels of ability or prior attainment, but unlike Scotland's Higher Still it is not designed as a progression ladder. This means, for example, that a student who has achieved a WelshBac at Foundation or General level is not seen as progressing to a WelshBac at General or Advanced level. Nor would the WelshBac, with its strong emphasis on a holistic provision for teenagers, be likely to appeal to adults. We think it would be relatively easy to address this issue by conceiving the WelshBac in terms of two conceptual levels: units of curriculum and assessment, and rules for combining units and modules. Most of the units (except perhaps the core studies) could be available to students of all ages; the combination rules would apply only to young people. Students who wished to upgrade their WelshBac could take the relevant units at a higher level. Such a developmental approach, of course, would require that the elements of the WelshBac are developed incrementally and in a way which accommodates the needs of all potential learners. Such revisions would put the WelshBac proposals in a good position to influence how Welsh policy makers tackle the question of overarching certification.

This brings us to the second issue, the change strategy behind the proposals for a WelshBac. As suggested earlier, the proposals appear to reject incrementalism and go for a 'big bang' approach to qualification reform. The WelshBac begins with a large vision (a holistic curriculum framework) and then considers the curriculum units needed to realise the vision. Yet developments elsewhere in Welsh education, such as CREDIS and the 'seamless' qualifications framework proposed in *Learning is for Everyone,* reflect the opposite strategy: an incremental approach which starts by developing a framework of units as a basis for a vision. The problem with these latter developments, like the parallel ones in England, is that they tend to be seen by practitioners as 'small steps' lacking any sense of purpose or direction. Experience both in England and Scotland suggests that although systemic change must be incremental, a policy based on incremental changes also needs a clear vision of where it is going (Spours & Young, 1996; Raffe & Howieson, 1998). In our view the WelshBac offers such a vision of the future for Wales. Though it may not be accepted by all, it could be as a vision to guide incremental change rather than as an alternative to replace existing qualifications, that the WelshBac proposals have a role to play in shaping Welsh policy for post-compulsory education in the future.

### Conclusions

This chapter has reviewed recent policy developments for unifying academic and vocational learning in Wales in light of lessons from our Anglo-Scottish comparisons. Our conclusions must remain tentative; at the time of writing, in 1998, it is not possible to predict the impact of the National Assembly for Wales or the influence on Assembly policy of the work of the Education and Training Action Group. We identified the constraints of Wales sharing a qualifications system with England and of the large flow between the two countries of those obtaining jobs and places in higher education, and examined three possible responses: reforms that focus on dimensions of unification other than qualifications, including reforms of government and qualification bodies and local institutions; reforms within the existing qualifications system; and reforms that develop alternative qualifications. We described developments in official policy that illustrate the first two of these responses and we examined proposals for a new qualification, the WelshBac, which exemplifies the third and represents a direct challenge to recent official policy.

Our Anglo-Scottish research, and the fact that English and Welsh qualifications are likely to remain inextricably linked, raise doubts as to whether the WelshBac with its 'big bang' approach to qualification reform is likely to be adopted in its present form. On the other hand, the WelshBac proposals could have an important role in shaping policy developments in Wales and, in particular, the way in which the proposals for a single qualification framework in the recent Green Paper are interpreted. The WelshBac could provide a vision of the aims of a future system for Wales and give a clearer direction to the proposed development of a credit-based framework for lifelong learning.

Despite the greater similarities between Welsh and English reform strategies than we found when comparing Scotland and England, there are areas where Welsh strategies are distinctively different from those being adopted in England. In particular, Welsh policy makers are giving priority to the development of a national credit framework and a single unit-based system of funding for all post-16 students. Although Wales shares a qualification system with England, the existence of a credit framework in Wales which runs parallel with traditional qualifications means that the two countries differ on the dimension of certification. However, a credit framework alone, when the existing tracked qualification system remains in place, is only one component of a linkages strategy; other measures would be needed, such as a system of overarching certification to encourage students to combine units from different qualifications. Nevertheless, in making the decision to establish a post-16 credit framework, educational policy in Wales holds significantly greater potential for movement towards a unified system than any of the reforms that are currently proposed in England.

*Acknowledgements*

This chapter is a product of the Unified Learning Project, funded by the UK Economic and Social Research Council (L123251039) as part of its programme on The Learning Society. We are grateful to Mike Jones, Linda Badham, John Howells, John David and John Osmond for their comments on an earlier draft of this paper. The final version of the chapter, however, remains our responsibility.

### References

Beaumont, G. (1996) *Review of 100 NVQs and SVQs*. London: DfEE.

Cramphorn, J., Richardson, W., Spours, K., Woolhouse, J., & Young, M. (1997) *Learning for the Future Final Report*. London: Post-16 Education Centre, Institute of Education, University of London and Centre for Education and Industry, University of Warwick.

David, J. & Jenkins, C. (1996) *The Welsh Baccalaureate Cymru*. Cardiff: Institute of Welsh Affairs (IWA).

David, J. & Jenkins, C. (1997) *The Welsh Baccalaureate. Matching International Standards. IWA Discussion, Paper No 2*. Cardiff: IWA.

Dearing, R. (1996) *Review of Qualifications for 16–19 Year Olds*. Hayes: SCAA Publications.

Delamont, S. & Rees, G. (1997) *Understanding the Welsh Education System: does Wales need a separate 'policy sociology'? Working Paper 23*. Cardiff: Department of Education, University of Wales, Cardiff.

Department for Education and Employment (DfEE) (1997) *Qualifying for Success: a consultative paper on the future of post-16 qualifications*. Sudbury: DfEE.

DfEE (1998a) Qualifying for Success: the response to the Qualifications and Curriculum Authority's advice, letter from Baroness Blackstone, Minister of State to Sir William Stubbs, Chairman, Qualifications and Curriculum Authority, DfEE, 3 April.

DfEE (1998b) *The Learning Age*. Cm3790. London: The Stationery Office.

Department of Education and Science/Welsh Office(1988) *Advancing A Levels* (Higginson Report). London: HMSO.

Fforwm (1997) *CREDIS: a learning route for Wales*. The Report of the Wales Modularisation and Credit based Development Project, October 1993–March 1997. Cardiff: Fforwm.

Finegold, D., Keep, E., Miliband, D., Raffe, D., Spours, K. & Young, M. (1990) *A British Baccalauréat?* London: IPPR.

Further Education Unit (1992) *A Basis for Credit*. London: FEU.

Gorard, S. (1997) *A Brief History of Education and Training in Wales 1900–1996. Working Paper 4, Project on Patterns of Participation in Adult Education and Training*. Cardiff: University of Wales, Cardiff.

Howieson, C., Raffe, D., Spours, K. & Young, M. (1997) Unifying Academic and Vocational Learning: the state of the debate in England and Scotland, *Journal of Education and Work*, 10, pp. 5–35.

Howieson, C., Raffe, D., Spours, K. & Young, M. (1998) *Group Awards, Over-arching Certification and the Unification of Academic and Vocational Learning. Working Paper 6, Unified Learning Project*. London: Universities of Edinburgh and London.

Institute of Welsh Affairs (1993) *Wales 2010: creating our future*. Cardiff: IWA.

Institute of Welsh Affairs (1994) *Towards an Educational Policy for Wales*. Cardiff: IWA.

Jenkins, C., David, J., Osmond, J. & Pierce, J. (1997) *The WelshBac: educating Wales in the next century*. Cardiff: IWA.

Jones, G. (1997) *The Education of a Nation*. Cardiff: University of Wales Press.

Lasonen, J. & Young, M. (Eds) (1998) *Strategies for Achieving Parity of Esteem in European Upper Secondary Education*. Jyväskylä: Institute for Educational Research, University of Jyväskylä.

Pritchard Jones, E. & David, J. (1997/98) The WelshBac and the Government's Proposals Compared, *Agenda* (IWA), winter, pp. 42–43.

Raffe, D. (1997) Upper Secondary Education, in M. Clark & P. Munn (Eds) *Education in Scotland: from pre-school to primary*. London: Routledge.

Raffe, D. (1998) Does Learning Begin at Home? The Place of 'Home International' Comparisons in UK Policy-making, *Journal of Education Policy*, 13, pp. 591–602.

Raffe, D. Arnman, G. & Bergdahl, P. (1998a) The Strategy of a Unified System, in J. Lasonen & M. Young (Eds) (1998) *Strategies for Achieving Parity of Esteem in European Upper Secondary Education*. Jyväskylä: Institute for Educational Research, University of Jyväskylä.

Raffe, D. & Howieson, C. (1998) The Higher Still Policy Process, *Scottish Affairs*, 24, pp. 90–108.

Raffe, D. Howieson, C. Spours, K. & Young, M. (1998b) The Unification of Post-compulsory Education: towards a conceptual framework, *British Journal of Educational Studies*, 46, pp. 169–187.

Raffe, D. & Lasonen, J. (1998) Comparison of Post-16 Strategies to Promote Parity of Esteem between Vocational and General Education in Europe, paper presented to CEDEFOP/DIPF Conference on Comparative Vocational Education and Training Research in Europe, January, Bonn.

Rees, G. (1997) The Educational Policy Process in Wales, paper presented to Scottish Educational Policy Forum seminar on The Educational Policy Processes of the UK, October, Edinburgh.

Scottish Office (1994) *Higher Still: opportunity for all*. Edinburgh: Scottish Office.

Scottish Office Education Department (1983) *16–18s in Scotland: an action plan*. Edinburgh: SED.

Spours, K. & Young, M. (1996) Dearing and Beyond: steps and stages to a unified 14–19 qualifications system? *British Journal of Education and Work*, 9(3), pp. 5–18.

Spours, K. Young, M. Howieson, C. & Raffe, D. (1998) *Regulation, Awarding Bodies and the Process of Unification in England and Scotland. Unified Learning Project Working Paper 4.* Edinburgh: Universities of Edinburgh and London.

Welsh Office (1997) *Building Excellent Schools Together,* Cm 3701. London: The Stationery Office.

Welsh Office (1998) *Learning is for Everyone.* Cm 3924. London: The Stationery Office.

Young, M., Spours, K., Howieson, C. & Raffe, D. (1997) Unifying Academic and Vocational Learning and the Idea of a Learning Society, *Journal of Education Policy*, 12, pp. 527–537.

# Scottish Education: myths and mists

## DAVID MATHESON

### Introduction

This aim of this chapter is to describe, discuss and offer analysis of Scottish formal education, a topic which, like so many others in life in general and in education in particular, has its own sets of myths, misunderstandings and misconceptions. The Scots, as we shall see, not only create and sustain their own myths but have them reinforced by misconceptions held elsewhere in the United Kingdom (UK). Various sources of evidence for the truth or otherwise of the selected myths are examined and reasons sought for their establishment and sustenance. Given that the Scots tend very frequently to define themselves with respect to the English (and given that all too many writers subsume Scotland into England), much emphasis is given to points of similarity and difference between these two countries and systems.

### Scotland

Before we can begin to discuss Scottish education in any of its guises, we first have to define what Scotland is. From a Scottish viewpoint, this is difficult enough as we shall see shortly. From an English viewpoint, the difficulties can magnify to an enormous extent. There is, for example, the tendency in England to refer to cities such as Manchester as being in the North. As such, a non connoisseur of UK geography could be forgiven for believing that the country more or less ended at Manchester or thereabouts. This being so, where does that put the Northern English areas of Cumbria and Northumberland. More importantly, for our present needs, where does such an attitude put the whole of Scotland? Interestingly, for the Scots, the 'south' means England. All geographical markers are of course relative. What is important is the use made of them, by whom and in which contexts. As Breitenbach et al (1998) put it:

> *How many book titles use the word 'British'? How many of them use it*
> *justifiably? The phenomenon is seen at its worst in instances of historical*
> *amnesia that allow English commentators [during the 1994 World*
> *Cup] still to consider the Republic of Ireland as part of the UK. ... If an*
> *independent nation can still be subsumed into Britain in so many*
> *consciousnesses, it is perhaps hardly surprising that Scotland, still part*
> *of the Union, fails to emerge as a distinct and separate identity.*
> *(pp. 49–50)*

The problem is not helped by the name of the country. The immediate question which follows is to ask which country one is referring to. The UK must be about the only country in the world which is unsure about its name. The USA might term itself America but each term means exactly the same thing. This is not the case for the terms used often interchangeably for the UK. As Tom Nairn (1988) puts it:

> *None of the existing handles quite fit: we live in a State with a variety*
> *of titles having different functions and nuances – the UK (or 'Yookay',*
> *as Raymond Williams relabelled it), Great Britain (imperial robes),*
> *Britain (boring lounge-suits), England (poetic but troublesome), the*
> *British Isles (too geographical), 'This Country' (all-purpose within the*
> *Family), or 'This Small Country of Ours' (defensive Shakespeare).*
> *(p. 93)*

UK is not, as Nigel Grant (1997) likes to remind us, synonymous with Great Britain. Still less is it synonymous with England. Nonetheless these terms change places regularly, albeit with the prefix Anglo now tending to be used more and England for the UK being used less, at least in the media. This is underlined by White's (1996) assertion that 'The English have never really distinguished Englishness from Britishness' (p. 337). And, as if to demonstrate the truth of his assertion the same writer then goes on to discuss the National Curriculum as if it referred to the whole of the UK and not just England and Wales (pp. 338–342). As we shall see below, it does not.

Until recently, even the passports for this country did not accurately use its name. They may have said UK passport on the front, but they were termed British inside, the country referred to as GB; a reference which entirely ignored the Northern Irish who, however much they may want it, are strictly speaking not British. They are *UK-ite*!

For the Scots themselves there are various 'Us and Them' scenarios which are played out. There is for example the generalised, though perhaps decreasing, tendency for the Scots to define themselves by contrast with their perception of the English. There are also tendencies for the Highlanders to define themselves by contrast with the Lowlanders. Edinburgh and Glasgow set themselves in opposition to one another. There are religious differences whose effect is mercifully on the decline as football becomes less associated with religion but Scotland is also linguistically and culturally fragmented:

Scotland has two indigenous languages, namely Scots and Gaelic, and a multitude of recent immigrant languages. One thing which all these languages share, to a greater or lesser extent, is the use of words from English and division into various dialects. Scots developed in parallel with what would become English and is descended from a dialect of Northumbrian. Contrary to what many Scots seem to believe, it is not English but a language related to it in just the same way as Danish and Norwegian are related:

> *The linguistic ancestor of Scots was a blend of Old English and Old*
> *Norse as spoken by the inhabitants of Northern England between the*
> *time of the first Viking invasions of around AD800 and the Norman*
> *Conquest of 1066. (Corbett, 1997, p. 4)*

Despite the antiquity of their mother tongue, the attitude which is prevalent in Scotland towards Scots is one of generalised disparagement. It is a language of quaint romanticism or of comedy. Never is it regarded as a language for use where content is more important than medium. (Grant & Docherty, 1992, p. 153). The real differences between the two are neatly illustrated by McClure (1988):

> *The Spanish ambassador at the court of James IV reported to his*
> *master that the King's Scots was as different from English as Aragonese*
> *(i.e. Catalan) from Castilian. (p. 28)*

It is the similarity of Scots to English which has been a major factor in its downfall to its present state of fragmentation, compounded by the almost inevitably close relations between the two countries. The Union of the Crowns in 1603 took the Royal Court of Scotland from Edinburgh to London, which signified the transfer of the seat of power, removed at a stroke a major impetus for the sustenance of native culture and seemed to have served in many Scottish minds to highlight a notion of superiority of English culture over Scots.

Such was the closeness of English and Scots that the translation of the Bible into English in the Authorised Version of King James was readable by the Scots. In the Enlightenment the call of London was generally too much for the Scottish intelligentsia of the Enlightenment to resist: writers such as Hume sent their manuscripts south to have every trace of 'Scotticisms' removed. Indeed Hume employed a butcher in Southend for this task. These writers may have spoken Scots but they would strenuously avoid writing in it (Kay, 1986). The decline of Scots continued unabated from the eighteenth century onwards and what was once a major literary language in Europe is now very often stigmatised as 'Bad English'. Yet as McClure (1988) makes clear:

> *'Bad English' ... is what is spoken by, let us say, an adult foreign*
> *learner with an imperfect knowledge of the language, making mistakes*

*which he presumably would avoid if he could: Scots, a speech form*
*existing in its own right, is not to be likened to this. (pp. 16–17)*

McClure's views are far from universally held, even (or perhaps most especially) among the Scots. For many of them, Scots is simply a dialect of English or merely a regional variation or, worse yet, just bad English. Scots is broken into dialects but then so are most European languages. And yet this situation is held up as 'proof' that Scots is a mere regional variant of English. Is this sufficient reason to exclude Scots from the list of 'real' languages? As Montgomery (1986) puts it, 'Questions such as "What counts as a language?" "How does a dialect become the standard?" are ultimately political and social as well as linguistic questions' (p. 186). Indeed, if we are to exclude Scots from those forms of speech which exist as languages in their own right, we should without hesitation exclude Danish, Norwegian and Swedish. We should consider Czech and Slovak as one tongue. The fact that this does not happen is perhaps a reflection of where the political and cultural power lie.

For its part, Gaelic has always had the status of language, even if it were sometimes referred to as Irish or *Ersch*. Nonetheless it has hardly had an easy time. Attacked ruthlessly following the 1745 Rebellion (which many Scots still see as a fight for Scottish nationhood rather than an attempted *putsch* against the UK crown), Gaelic was increasingly marginalised until recently. The creation in 1891 of An Comunn Gaidhlealach (The Gaelic Association) whose main aim was to establish a Gaelic Festival along the lines of the *Eisteddfod*, a Welsh reinvention of an ancient Druid ritual which was reborn in the nineteenth century as a celebration of Welsh language and culture. In the 1982 *An Comunn Gaidhlealach* in association with various other bodies founded *Comunn na Gàidhlig* (CNAG) as the national development agency for Scottish Gaelic which has been instrumental in encouraging the establishment of Gaelic medium education at all levels. Additionally there has been much agitation from parents demanding that their MPs support Gaelic education. The net result is that the number of Gaelic medium units in primary schools has steadily grown from 2 in 1984 to 47 in 1994, with the number of children involved rising over the same period from 24 to over 1200 (*Thig a Theasag,* 1995). However, especially at secondary school level, teachers are scarce and the future of Gaelic medium secondary school is threatened by Her Majesty's Inspectorate of Schools who, whilst praising the quality of Gaelic-medium primary schools and primary bilingual units (*Provision for Gaelic Education in Scotland,* 1994), now feel that Gaelic-medium secondary schooling should be crammed into a single cultural course (*Cothrom 10*). This proposal is being vigorously opposed by all the Gaelic organisations, including the politically very active *Comunn nam Pàrant* (The Parents' Association). Time will tell whether Gaelic's current revival through education can continue. Languages in more precarious positions, such as Faeroese, have been brought back from the brink of extinction through the use of education. We shall have to wait and see if Gaelic can do the same.

Scottish culture is itself seen as being divided and ill-defined. (McCrone, 1996) This perception, well-illustrated by the works of Sir Walter Scott, is that of a Scotland torn between the 'heart' representing the past and Scottish society, and the 'head' representing the present, the future, the intellect and the British State. This 'split personality', which Smith (1919 in Osmond, 1988) terms the *Caledonian Antisyzygy*, is a division between the Scottish 'heart' and the British 'head' and is 'one of the most common characterisations of Scotland.' (McCrone, 1996, p. 175) It is rooted in the Scottish tradition of thinking and speaking one language whilst writing another whose inevitable consequence is a type of neurosis in the collective consciousness.

It is against this backdrop that we can now look at Scottish education.

### Scotland and England: some similarities and differences

As in England, Scottish children start school at about age 5. Unlike England, there is rarely a hard and fast cut-off dates for the so-called 'rising fives', i.e. children have not yet reached the age of five but who are judged (usually on the basis of available places) to be sufficiently mature as to be able start primary school. This difference in attitude can lead to problems when a child educated in Scotland moves to England. The Scottish child may have completed, say, six years of primary school but, if the birthday falls after the English cut-off date, the parent may have some persuading to do if s/he wants the child to avoid repeating the sixth year.[1] The Scots always have to do seven years of primary school and there are no middle schools as compared to the English having, in general, six years of primary except where there are middle schools.

At secondary school the structural differences continue with the Scots not only able to leave after only four years (at age 16) but also able to sit examinations which can lead to university entrance at age 17. Few English pupils, usually only the exceptionally gifted, have this opportunity. Times are changing however in Scotland. As secondary schools' finances depend increasingly on keeping pupils in the upper part of school for as long as possible, there is a growing tendency to discourage pupils from the fifth year from moving on to university, regardless of the exam success. This, as we shall see, is having its effect on the width of the Scottish upper secondary curriculum.

Scottish universities also have their structural differences with their English counterparts: the Scottish Ordinary degree is not, usually, a failed Honours degree as it often is perceived in England. It is a general degree, one which leaves specialisation for the world of work. It is a qualification which suffers from misrepresentation and misunderstanding, even within its native country. An Honours degree in Scotland lasts four years as opposed to three in England. Until recently, it was common practice in many of Scotland's universities for students to take an Ordinary degree before proceeding to Honours. There is a certain romanticism attached to the Ordinary degree and among the greater exponents of this is George Davie, best known for his book *The Democratic Intellect* (1961). Over the years the Ordinary degree has declined in both popularity and importance although it is notable that Glasgow University has relaunched the concept in an attempt officially to revive the tradition. Perhaps the revival is as much a recognition of the changing nature of the student body. Nonetheless the true value attached in Scotland to this 'tradition' is perhaps best shown by the fact that until the 1970s, a teacher in Scotland who did not have an Honours degree could not be promoted. The perceived 'higher' level of the Honours graduates was such that not only could they apply for promotion but they even had their own professional association in the shape of the Scottish Secondary Teachers' Association.

At the legal level, there are substantive differences between Scottish and English schools. First, there is no National Curriculum in Scotland. Whether this is for better or for worse is another issue but the Scottish Office Education and Industry Department (SOEID) (now the Scottish Executive Education Department) has only ever issued guidelines on the curriculum, never prescriptions. This has maintained, at least to some extent, a feeling that the relationship between central and local government of education is one of partnership rather than one of centralised authority exerting its will where it likes (McPherson & Raffe, 1988). Scotland has no Office for Standards in Education (OFSTED) but rather has maintained Her Majesty's Inspectorate of Schools (HMI) as the only body which can inspect schools. While OFSTED inspections usually include so-called 'lay people', HMI visits are always conducted by civil servants. Scotland possesses a General Teaching Council (GTC), modelled on the General Medical Council, which controls entrance to the school teaching profession. The GTC allows decides who can teach what in secondary schools. It insists, to within a few exceptions especially in areas of relative geographical isolation, that all secondary teachers be formally qualified to a sufficient level (decided by the GTC itself) in all subjects they propose to teach. This has major ramifications on the economic viability of smaller secondary schools who may find themselves threatened with closure as much through the need to maintain a large complement of teachers as through falling school rolls. It militates against initiatives such as mini-schools wherein a large school is effectively broken up into autonomous sub-units and which has been used to some success in, for example, the USA in a bid to reduce antisocial behaviour in school. (Meighan & Siraj-Blatchford, 1998) It also has tended to entrench even further the subject basis of the Scottish secondary school curriculum. If one were to introduce a programme of study which crossed subject boundaries, one has the immediate quandary of how to satisfy the GTC requirements as to teacher qualification unless one begins from the standpoint that different parts of the programme would be taught under different subject headings and hence by different subject specialists. The ossification of the curriculum is evident and arguably delivers a clear message to learners that knowledge as such is divided according to specialisms. This said, from the practising secondary teacher's viewpoint there are some advantages in the GTC's rigidity: one cannot be required to teach a subject just because one is known, or suspected, to have some competence in it.

The power of the GTC is not to be underestimated. It is extremely difficult to fire a teacher in Scotland. However, a report to the GTC can result in a disciplinary hearing, a consequence of which may be removal from the Teaching Register. The teacher is thus not actually fired but it becomes illegal to employ him/her in a state school in Scotland. The powers of the GTC are enshrined in law and it has stood up to central government on many occasions. Unlike England, Scotland has no Teacher Training Agency, the result of resistance by the GTC to an attempt at eroding its powers. The actual council of the GTC is elected mainly by teachers, whose representatives form a majority but it also includes representatives of local and central government and of higher education. In their self-government and self-regulation, the teachers in Scotland arguably are more professional than that of England. Also enshrined in law in Scotland is the maximum number of children that can be in a classroom at any one time. In primary school and in non-practical subjects in secondary this is limited to 33 pupils but if the class in composite (i.e. covering more than one year of primary), the number permitted drops to 26. At the time of massive industrial action throughout schools in the UK in the early 1970s, the teachers' unions in England and Wales accepted what might best be described as a gentleman's agreement on class sizes which was later breached. Their Scottish counterparts held out for an article of law which has never been repealed, government threats to do so being withdrawn after counter-threats from the sometimes quite bellicose Scottish teachers' unions. We should note that the notion of union as it applies to teachers in Scotland can be slightly misleading. The largest teachers union in Scotland, the Educational Institute of Scotland (EIS), is strictly speaking a professional association but it also has the power to grant its own teaching qualifications, a power which is almost never used but which in the 19th century gave one of the few degree-level teaching qualifications available in Scotland, the Licentiate of the Educational Institute of Scotland. This compares in some ways to the Licentiate granted by the College of Teachers (formerly the College of Preceptors) in England and Wales although, unlike the EIS, the College of Teachers has never developed its role to represent teachers in their day-to-day business. Like the College of Teachers, the EIS still elects Fellows occasionally.

Both north and south of the Border there has been a delegation of budgets to schools. In England and Wales this delegation goes as far as teachers' salaries. It can be very advantageous financially for a school in

England and Wales to employ inexperienced and hence cheaper teachers rather than to employ a teacher at the top of the salary scale. In Scotland, the salary budget is paid out of funds held by the local authority (incidentally Scotland, unlike England and Wales, does not and never has had Local Education Authorities *per se*), the school being responsible for the non-pay budget. It therefore makes no financial difference for a school in Scotland to employ a new entrant to the profession or an old hand.

Unlike England and Wales, Scotland has no school governors as such. Michael Forsyth in his days as Minister for Education at the Scottish Office attempted to introduce School Boards (following a brief visit to Denmark where he seems to have largely misunderstood Danish School Boards which operate on a basis of consensus). The 1988 School Boards (Scotland) Act followed and schools were required to establish Boards within a short time span. Many succeeded in doing so but virtually none of these Boards have ever sought to widen their powers from sitting on selection committees for senior management and offering general advice to headteachers. School Boards in Scotland have no role in school discipline whether as regards staff or pupils. They cannot fire staff and have no say over pupil exclusions or suspensions. Parents of suspended pupils can appeal to the local education committee but they can no more than voice concerns to the School Board who may note these and pass them on to the headteacher but cannot take any other action except to perhaps discuss discipline in general.

At the time of the establishment of School Boards the Conservative government believed that Scottish parents (who have an in-built majority on the Boards and a Board cannot be quorate unless there are a majority of parents present) would seize the chance for power and would sweep schools towards self-government.[2] This *opting-out* would mean the Board and school leaving local authority control and being funded directly from central government. In the 10 years that opting-out was available, few schools sought self-government, always because they were under threat of closure and only one, Dornoch Academy, succeeded in leaving local authority control. One might reasonably surmise that Scottish parents are content with their local authorities, at least as far as schools are concerned, or that they are just too apathetic. The low rate of uptake of places on School Boards might suggest the latter. There are seldom elections for School Boards as the number of candidates is usually too low.

The power of parents in Scotland was aptly demonstrated when the government attempted in the early 1990s to introduce national tests for children at ages 7, 11 and 14. Initially children in each cohort were all to be tested on the same day. The teachers' unions and the Scottish School Boards Association (SSBA) protested: the former on the grounds that teachers' professionalism was being undermined; the latter on the grounds that children should not be subjected to formal tests on an arbitrary date but rather, if they were to be tested at all, it should be at a moment when the teacher judged the child best ready. Government persisted. The unions initially asked their members to boycott the tests, a point which ran into difficulties over the terms of teachers' contracts, and finally the SSBA and the Scottish Association of Parent Teachers Association suggested to parents that their child might be 'sick' on the day of the test. In face of massive pupil absence, the government backed down, the unions accepting the principle of the tests but winning the major victory of teachers being able to decide when the tests would take place for each child. The tests planned for age 14 were forgotten.

Just as few Scottish schools sought to opt-out, unlike in England and Wales, so is it that few Scottish children attend private schools (Benn & Chitty, 1997). It is worth mentioning in passing that in Scotland a public school means just that: it is a school in the state sector, open to the public. Any school not in the state sector in Scotland is private, despite the attempts by some private schools in Edinburgh to style themselves 'Public' to reflect what they perceive as their English counterparts.[3] The fact that few Scottish private schools, even in Edinburgh, are residential while the English Public schools generally are seems to have been overlooked.

Scotland took to comprehensive schools in a manner rarely repeated in England (Benn & Chitty, 1997) but what was conceived of as comprehensive covered a vast array of school and curriculum types. Certainly, in 1969 when I entered a so-called comprehensive school we were strictly separated into streams from day one and in those streams we largely stayed. When I returned to that school on teaching practice in the 1978, mixed-ability teaching took place for the first two years before children were put into sets for most subjects. I would argue that in my day the school was definitely not comprehensive except as far as the front door. Once inside, it was as rigidly selective as had been the case in the days of more overt selection.

Lastly in this section, a few terms: the Scots do not take GCSE exams like their English cousins. Rather they have Standard Grade, administered by a single examinations board, the Scottish Qualifications Authority (SQA), in contrast with the several that administer GCSE. An examination of GCSE syllabi and those of Standard Grade shows that they are generally identical. What distinguishes, say, GCSE Maths and Standard Grade Maths are differences of detail, not of substance. What does cause confusion is that the English grade their GCSE from A* to E, with A* being the highest grade, while the Scots grade their Standard Grade from 1 to 7 with 1 being the best. While the English have their 'traditional' A Level, which actually only dates from 1950, for university entrance, the Scots have Higher Grade, a certificate whose name dates from the nineteenth century. Until the 1950s university-bound pupils in Scotland might have attempted 3 Highers and 3 Lowers at one sitting in the then block exam. Lowers were abolished to be replaced with Ordinary Grade (which the Scots frequently called O-Levels and mixed them up with their English equivalents), to be taken at around age 16 and these in turn were replaced by Standard Grade from 1988 onwards.

Higher Grade, as presently conceived, consists of the work load of about half the corresponding A Level but the work is carried out over less than one school year. Indeed if we allow for the time generally given for revision and the fact that Higher Grade exams occur in May (with schools starting in August) then we find half an A Level being done in about one third of the time. Pupils also tend to do more subjects at Higher than they would do at A Level. The result appears to be a greater workload, a point easily overlooked by university admissions tutors who may only be aware of the apparent equivalencies between the products of these courses rather than the processes followed.[4] The current relaunch of A/S level in England whereby it becomes effectively an English version of the Higher to be taken before pupils move on to study A Levels over one year could have interesting ramifications and *perhaps* move towards increasing understanding between the systems, provided, of course, that A/S is recognised as being more or less a Higher. There exists a Scottish qualification of roughly A Level standard, this being the Certificate of Sixth Year Studies (CSYS) which was never meant to be a university entrance exam but is increasingly becoming just that. It differs however from A Level in that in most CSYS courses the pupil is required to undertake an extended piece of independent research and there is only limited emphasis on the terminal exam. At the time of writing, moves are afoot to replace Higher Grade with Higher and CSYS with Advanced Higher, both these innovations being hailed as attempts to bridge to academic-vocational divide which currently is seen to exist. The new *Higher Still* programme allows a larger variety of entry and exit points than before and aims to cater effectively for all levels of pupil accomplishment. It is composed of short courses (National Units) which, if taken in particular groupings together with an external assessment, form National Courses. A balanced programme of National Courses and National Units forms a Scottish Group Award and this is available at five levels, ranging from the most basic (*Access*) through Higher to the new Advanced Higher. Candidates can in theory move from one level to the next upon successful completion of the first (SQA, 1998). The potential for utter confusion is immense. As with Standard Grade before it, the SQA and SEED seem determined to introduce the new courses as fast as possible. There has been no real piloting (if indeed any at all). There was a brief consultation period before course writers were commissioned to produce the syllabi. It goes almost without saying that the teachers and their unions predict a similar farce to that which accompanied the first attempts at Standard Grade: courses were far too long; assessment was grossly overcomplicated; administration was a nightmare; no-one seemed to understand what the new courses were about, be they teachers, parents, pupils or employers. Eventually Standard Grades were revamped as simpler but workable structures and have generally proved popular (despite still being referred to on occasions as O-Levels!) In a declared attempt to avoid repeating the experiences of the launch of Standard Grade, the EIS initially boycotted the development of the Higher Still programme but is now cooperating fully.

| | Scotland | England |
|---|---|---|
| **starting age** | around 5: very loose notion of what constitutes around 5 | around 5: strict cut-off date |
| **school structure** | primary for seven years then secondary for at least four years | primary school for six years then secondary for at least five years; various other systems of lower, middle and upper school |
| **school inspection** | HMI (civil servants only) | OFSTED (includes lay members) |
| **class sizes** | legal max. 33 up to age 16; 26 in composite classes; 20 in practical classes | no maximum (but action promised by government) |
| **school budgets** | all but salaries | include salaries |
| **school governance** | weak School Boards, aid in selection of senior staff, no role in discipline of staff or pupils | strong Governors, role in hiring and firing of staff, and in discipline of staff and pupils |
| **entrance to teaching** | GTC lays down conditions; government advises. | TTA lays down conditions, follows government instructions. |
| **selective state schools** | none | in some areas |
| **curriculum** | 5-14 *Guidelines:* advisory only | National Curriculum: government prescriptions |
| **who can teach what in secondary school** | to within some geographical exceptions, teachers must be qualified in the subject to be taught | now there's a question |
| **national tests** | at age 7, 11: administered at teacher's discretion | at age 7, 11, 14: administered when QCA decides |
| **16+** | Standard Grade | GCSE |
| **17+** | Higher Grade | new A/S Level |
| **18+** | more Highers; CSYS; new Advanced Highers | A-Level |
| **university** | 3 years ordinary degree; 4 years honours; SHEFC funding | 3 years honours degree; HEFCE funding |

**Table 1: Formal Education Scotland and England: some similarities and differences**

| | |
|---|---|
| CSYS | Certificate of Sixth Year Studies |
| GCSE | General Certificate of Secondary Education |
| GTC | General Teaching Council |
| HEFCE | Higher Education Funding Council for England |
| HMI | Her Majesty's Inspectorate of Schools |
| OFSTED | Office for Standards in Education |
| QCA | Qualifications and Curriculum Authority |
| SHEFC | Scottish Higher Education Funding Council |
| TTA | Teacher Training Agency |

| age | stage | events |
|---|---|---|
| 5 | start primary | |
| 7 | | national tests |
| 11 | | national tests |
| 12 | start secondary | |
| 16 | end of compulsory school | Standard Grade<br>*plus sometimes*<br>National Certificate modules |
| 17 | | Higher Grade<br>*&/or*<br>National Certificate modules;<br>possible entrance to HE |
| 18 | | Higher Grade *&/or*<br>CSYS *&/or*<br>National Certificate modules;<br>possible entrance to HE |
| 17/18+ | further/higher education | |

Note: Post-16 qualifications may also be followed in further education colleges. All apprenticeships are made up of National Certificate modules, generally validated by SQA but also sometimes by the City and Guilds of London Institute or other industry lead bodies.

Table II. Steps through formal education in Scotland.

## Scottish Myths and Misunderstandings

Like any other social grouping, Scottish education has its share of myths. My purpose here is to look at a few of these and discern if there is a basis in fact or if the myth is more fabrication or misremembering than anything else.

### The Width of the Curriculum

It is commonplace in Scotland to hear commentators and teachers waxing lyrical about the width of the Scottish school curriculum. The basis for this claim is hard to pin down but it seems to arise from a perception of school curricula in England, again a case of the Scots defining themselves with respect to, or by opposition to, the English. Certainly if we examine the number of subjects which *used to be taken* at Higher Grade, we find Scottish pupils who are university-bound studying up to six or seven subjects to be examined at the same level at one sitting. This compares with the two or three most of their English counterparts might follow. In this light, the

Scottish upper secondary school curriculum appears to be quite wide (although it looks rather limited when compared with many of those from the rest of Europe). However, two points have to be considered. The first concerns the attempts by secondary schools to get pupils to stay at school for a further year. The second concerns the curriculum further down the school.

On the first point, there is a growing tendency among secondary schools in Scotland to try to limit the number of Highers which a pupil might take at one sitting. This is presented to the pupil as being in his/her own interests, by maximising chances, reducing workload etc. Why pupils in the 1990s have problems coping with the workload their predecessors handled in the 1960s and 1970s remains a mystery. When one realises the parlous state of many schools' finances and the fact that their *per capita* allowance increases markedly for pupils in the sixth (and hence final) year, then a possible motivation for this strategy begins to reveal itself. The result now is that pupils are less encouraged to take the maximum number of Highers at one go but rather to split their Highers over the fifth and sixth years (possibly picking up a CSYS on the way). This lowering of expectations is, I feel, quite alarming. Lowered expectations lead to lowered results. Incidentally, those pupils who accept to only take three or so Highers in their fifth year are expected to fill up their timetable with National Certificate modules, also run by SQA and whose value is decidedly limited.[5]

While the Scottish curriculum at Higher Grade has certainly narrowed over the last 20 or so years, its width further down the school was never very great and this has not increased of late. The introduction of the National Curriculum in England and Wales caused much consternation among teachers in those countries. The amount of administration was criticised, often quite justifiably. Indeed, little was lauded by the teachers charged with the delivery of the Curriculum. In Scotland, teachers' unions congratulated themselves at having resisted such moves in their members' schools. Few things in life are absolutely good or absolutely bad and the National Curriculum is a fine mixture of positives and negatives. On the positive side is the removal from the teacher of the possibility of not teaching something simply because s/he does not like or cannot do it. In Scotland, this discretion is still available and is widely used. According to the 5–14 Guidance documents (5–14 being guidelines from the SOEID on what teachers should teach and at which level up to the beginning of Standard Grade courses), pupils should learn science from the first year of primary school. In fact, few pupils ever touch science in primary school. The reasons given vary from lack of expertise on the part of the teachers to lack of equipment on the part of the schools. Indeed, in my experience, primary teachers would often only teach science if a parent gave them some lessons and the materials to go with them. The situation is said to be improving but it has a long way to go.

That Scottish primary teachers are loath to introduce science underlines a myth that seems prevalent among them: namely, that science is hard to do and that it requires expensive equipment that is difficult to operate. Similar attitudes were common over IT equipment and these seem to have been dispelled. Perhaps time and the influx of entrants to the profession who have some science in their background will overcome this.

The legal status of the National Curriculum made such discretion more difficult to apply. Of course, from September 1998 the National Curriculum *requirements* have been radically reduced and teachers are only obliged to give due regard (whatever that might mean) to subjects other than those in the so-called core. Science is one of the core subjects but this is a select grouping that, in addition, only encompasses maths, English and Religious Education. One might be forgiven for wondering why the government has decided to tread such a path which brings England and Wales towards a Scottish model (as does the relaunch of A/S Level). An answer could lie in the number of Cabinet members educated in Scotland, coupled with the myth of Scottish excellence in education.

### The Myth of Scottish Excellence in Education

Given that the Scots tend to define themselves with respect to the English (or rather to their perception of the English) and take enormous pride in outdoing the English at anything, it is no surprise that they should decide that their education system is better than that of England. What is rather surprising is the extent to which such an attitude appears to be shared by the English.

Myths are not necessarily false. They are generally simplifications and/or distortions. They often have a basis in truth but sometimes a very selective or eclectic truth. The main problem is that they are irrational but believed (Bell & Grant, 1974). There is a certain smugness about the common way in which Scottish commentators all too often sound forth on the excellence in Scottish education (by which they mean schools primarily but may also encompass universities). Finding proof for the assertion is a wee bit harder to do. Indeed, examining Scotland nationally in a comparative context reveals few grounds for contentment with pupil achievement. In the Third International Mathematics and Science Survey little distinguishes the attainment of Scottish nine and 13-year-olds from those in England as far as mathematics are concerned, both England and Scotland achieved relatively low mean scores (NFER, 1998; Semple, 1998; TIMSS 1998a,b). At age nine and 13, England performed above average in Science while Scotland was above average at age nine and at the average at age 13. (TIMSS 1998a,b) If Scottish excellence at school had any real basis, then logically Scotland's children would produce test scores which, if not on par with highest scoring countries such as Singapore, would at least be well above average.

If we examine examination passes at Higher Grade we see the percentage of the cohort gaining three or more passes at grade C or better vary from less than 3% to over 90%. If we examine passes at Standard Grade, we see similar. There are 'good' schools and 'bad' schools. There are schools in deprived areas, such as All Saints Secondary in Glasgow, which outperform schools in more privileged areas, such as Lourdes Secondary, Glasgow. The whole gamut is there. By whatever measure one applies, there are some bits which are better than others. There are calm schools in wild areas and wild schools in calm areas. Despite the evidence that all human life is present in Scottish schools and that some parts seem to work better than others, the myth persists that simply by being Scottish, schools in Scotland are 'better' than those in England.

Notions such as this need to have deeper roots than simple chauvinism. They require some basis in fact or at least in tradition. They also need some reinforcement.

In the case of reinforcement, this arguably comes through the indirect intervention of the London-based media. Scottish education virtually never figures in the so-called national news on television (indeed Scotland does not figure very frequently either), neither does Scottish education appear much in London-based newspapers. On the other hand, viewers and readers are frequently regaled with tales of teachers being assaulted in English schools, pupils going on the rampage, the need for interventionist policies by government in inner city schools, and so on. If the grain of Scottish excellence is already planted (and it is a complete package including better behaved pupils), then the very absence of reporting of disturbances or low attainment or other negatives while giving much space to reporting negatives in English schools will serve to keep that grain growing. Absence of evidence to contradict the myth is easily taken as evidence favouring its continuance. In Scotland, the myth has been kept going by very limited reporting of disturbances in Scottish schools while viewers and readers regularly see tales of English schools in chaos. This is a paradoxical side to cultural imperialism. By largely ignoring Scottish culture and life in Scotland, the media serve to perpetuate a myth whereby the culturally submissive group appears superior.[6]

It is worth spending a moment looking at possible origins of the myth. Until the nineteenth century Scotland had four universities compared to England's two. Whether these could be termed centres of excellence is very much open to debate. Indeed Bell & Grant (1974) claim that it was only the advent of widespread student grants in the 1950s that made British universities centres of excellence for the first time. However, excellence is in the eye of the beholder so maybe there's some basis for the myth here. Perhaps a better starting point lies in the development of formal school systems. As Archer (1979) points out, before 1870 formal school systems were very much the exception. Indeed, among the few exceptions is the Central Lowlands of Scotland where a system of parish schools had slowly developed since the Reformation. It would be hard to imagine in eighteenth century England a ploughman's son becoming not only an Exciseman but also the national poet. Such a ploughman's son was Robert Burns, the very man who wrote that mastery of ethnocentrism: *wha's like us? Gie few an ther aw deid* [Who's like us? Very few and they're all dead].

Certainly literacy levels in Scotland seem to have been well above those in England up until at least the Balfour Act (1902) but equally important is perhaps the sheer number of these literate Scots who emigrated and so spread the belief that all Scots were literate. The Scots exported a disproportionate number of people into the armies and navies of the British Empire and into the colonial civil service and the East India Company. They were also disproportionately inventive, even though most of those who made any money out of their inventions had to do so outside of Scotland. Simply finding literate and inventive Scots scattered throughout the world might well have inclined observers to believe that there was something in Scottish education that made so many of them so learned.

Perhaps the perception of a greater degree of egalitarianism in Scottish education than in English has played its role and it is to this that we now turn.

### The Myth of Egalitarianism and the Lad o' Pairts

A theme which the writers of Kailyard [7] novels delighted in portraying was that of the poor lad, come down from village with a bag of meal over his shoulder to feed him for a term, set to make a success of the university. (It is perhaps relevant that the Scots simply speak of 'going to uni to *do* a subject' while the English may well speak of 'going up to varsity to *read* a subject'. These are certainly tiny differences but, without going in the direction of the Amazonian butterfly that flutters its wings and as a consequence there's a hurricane in Kent, the way in which we refer to a phenomenon of whatever variety will certainly affect our perceptions of it.) In the Kailyard version, the lad o' pairts had been spotted by his (it was always a boy) schoolmaster and groomed for greater things. The idea was a bit like the American dream, that all one had to do was to work hard and one could become a success from any station in life. The notion tied in with that expressed by Knox (1560) in the *First Book of Discipline* whereby children of talent would be nurtured at school and then sent to become ministers or doctors or enter some other respected profession. Kailyard was primarily written for consumption outside of Scotland and so could act as a perfect vehicle for propagating myths. In reality, lads o' pairts did exist. Unlike the Kailyard version, they were rarely from the poorest milieux but were rather what might now be termed middle-class (McCrone, 1996). What was also forgotten in Kailyard was that the schoolmaster, upon finding a lad o' pairts, might well abandon the rest of the class more or less to its own devices in order to groom the prodigy.

**Higher Education Institutions:** *Universities in italics*

| | | | |
|---|---|---|---|
| **Aberdeen** | *Aberdeen*<br>*Robert Gordon's*<br>Northern College | **Glasgow** | *Glasgow*<br>*Strathclyde*<br>*Glasgow Caledonian*<br>Glasgow School of Art<br>Royal Scottish Academy<br>of Music and Drama |
| **Dundee** | *Dundee*<br>*Abertay-Dundee*<br>Northern College | | |
| **Edinburgh** | *Edinburgh*<br>*Heriot Watt*<br>*Napier*<br>Edinburgh College of Art<br>Queen Margaret College | **Paisley** | *Paisley* |
| | | **Stirling** | *Stirling* |
| | | **St Andrews** | *St Andrews* |
| | | ***13 sites in the Highlands and Islands*** | University of Highlands<br>and Islands<br>*(from 2001)* |
| **Galashiels** | Scottish College of Textiles | | |

Figure 1. An educational map of Scotland.

Interestingly, although they do not really figure in the tales of lads o' pairts, the Highlands of Scotland have since the invention of the university sent a greater proportion of its young into higher education than any other part of the UK. This goes diametrically against international trends whereby rural and especially mountainous areas participate less than do urban areas. The answer to this apparent conundrum might lie in the traditional social structure of the Highlands. Based around common ownership of land, a group of families could send a child into higher education and still be able to work the land whereas had the land been an individual family's possession this could have caused insurmountable strains. Chronic under-employment in the Highlands has helped this trend continue. Indeed it was long recognised that the only way to get on was to get out (Matheson, 1992). This phenomenon could only serve to help the myth of social mobility through personal effort.

The fact remains however that Scottish universities are much more open to people from humble origins than were their English counterparts (McCrone, 1996). 'When social class is taken into account, 37% more Scots enter university education than would be expected on the basis of what happens in England and Wales' (Matheson, 1999). This is no new phenomenon since 'by the eve of the First World War, the proportion of the First World War, the proportion of working class students was as high at Glasgow as it was later in the twentieth century' (Anderson, 1983, p. 309). The role played by further education offering degree-level courses is also significant [8]: these being located in many more places than universities which, even now, are limited to the urban areas of the Central Belt and the East Coast. This leaves the greater part of the country with no direct contact with higher education (see Figure 1).

There is, of course, The Open University but, while this has consistently attracted students from across Scotland, its materials do not always take account of its being a UK organisation rather than an English one. Not taking account of receiving cultures is a frequent difficulty when an Open University seeks students from outwith its own country but one which should not occur when the University is in what is supposed to be its native land. However as far as the Highlands and Islands of Scotland are concerned, the problems of culture and of access to higher education in Scottish rural areas will soon be partially solved when the UK sees its first decentralised university in the shape of the University for the Highlands and Islands (UHI), a consortium of 13 existing colleges scattered over an area equal to one-fifth of the total surface of the UK, which hopes to receive its University Charter in 2001. Using the Internet, the UHI already offers franchised courses for institutions such as Aberdeen University and attracts interest from as far afield as Finland, Austria and Ireland (UHI, 21 August 1996). The creation of the UHI is the formalisation and culmination of the various franchise arrangements which have existed between the colleges and Aberdeen University for some years.

The creation of the UHI goes some way to redress the imbalance which has long existed in Scottish higher education whereby, despite having the highest age participation rate in the UK, the Highlands and Islands were denied a fixed site university both at the Robbins expansion and at the removal of the binary divide in 1992. Inverness already possessed a college of further and higher education which might have been developed beyond the few degree level courses it already offered. The UHI is in effect that development. Although the UHI will be an autonomous consortium, its students will be able to benefit from the well-developed credit transfer scheme which exists in Scotland. The country is well placed to move towards an integrated qualifications framework with 'every higher education institution ... signed up to the Scottish Credit and Transfer Scheme' (*The Times Higher Education Supplement,* 21 August 1998). This, in theory, at least enormously facilitates students moving between establishments.

**Conclusion**

It is arguably the case that every aspect of human society requires its myths. The reality of situations can be uncomfortable, even unbearable. Problems arise however when myths blind us completely to that reality. Myths can be useful to contextualise, to provide a backdrop. The danger is when they provide a fog. Scottish formal education is certainly a distinctive entity from that south of the border but, as we have seen, not as different as each might pretend. Neither are they as similar as those who subsume Scotland into England and equate the latter with the UK might imply. The two have their similarities, their good and bad points. They merit each the study by the other. Perhaps in this way, the Scots might realise that they have much to learn from the English, both in terms of lessons to follow and in terms of lessons to avoid. The English, for their part, might finally learn that lesson that Kenneth Baker never did: that there is no British education system [9], rather there are systems, mutually dependent in all manner of ways. The two might eventually learn to openly recognise the good points in each other. They already borrow heavily from each other in all sorts of ways: from common textbooks to syllabi that are almost identical. What they do not do is to recognise from where they are borrowing. The revamped A/S level is a Higher in disguise. The new Advanced Higher is effectively an A Level by another name. It goes beyond this, though, into fundamental concerns about social justice. Scotland is more open to economically deprived social classes in its entrance to higher education than is England. If the government wishes to generalise this trend to England, then some overt examination of how and why the Scots manage this is clearly called for. Baroness Blackstone (as Higher Education Minister) has called for less elitist A Levels to improve the chances of the working class of entering higher education (*The Daily Telegraph,* 18 September 1998). However she has not recognised that Scotland has already trod the path she wishes England to follow. Whether it be due to a more broadly-based upper secondary school, some factors of tradition or culture or some other effect, this difference between the two merits attention. Indeed, it could be that the solution to the conundrum lies in the creation of a fully-fledged Higher Level! How ironical therefore that as England questions the elitism of A Level, Scotland prepares to launch itself down that very path. There are none so blind as those who will not see. The Scots and the English, at least in terms of their school education systems, have just that blindness, a blatant refusal on all parts to acknowledge the educational development debt each owes to the other.

Perhaps the advent of the Scottish Parliament, with responsibility for all levels of education in Scotland, will help to change this situation. Time will tell.

## Notes

[1] Such was the case when my family moved from Glasgow to Northampton. As my son's birthday is on 12 September he was after the cut-off date and the LEA in Northampton wanted him to repeat the sixth year. Much persuasion and mention of the European Directive on the movement of migrant labour whereby the receiving system must adjust to the sending system was required before the problem was resolved and Ben could enter Year 7. The same arguments had to be re-used for him to enter Year 8. By the time he was due to enter Year 9, the administration in Northampton seemed to have adapted itself to this Scottish 'anomaly'.

[2] While Chairman and Training Organiser of Lourdes Primary School Board, Glasgow, from 1989 until 1991 when the Board folded due to no parent candidates presenting themselves at the mid-term elections, I attended many training events and discussion fora organised by the local authority (Strathclyde Regional Council), the Scottish School Boards Association and the Archdiocese of Glasgow. A point which was raised on many occasions over these two years was a deep suspicion that the government's creation of School Boards was simply an encouragement of apparent decentralisation from the local authority which would lead to actual centralisation directly under the Scottish Office.

[3] The attempts at Anglicisation by some parts of Edinburgh society, especially in the nineteenth century, are described in some detail in Bell & Grant (1977).

[4] See SQA (1998) *Comparability Study of Scottish Qualifications and GCE Advanced Level,* which manages to completely overlook the workload aspect of comparing Highers and A Levels.

[5] During an industrial placement at Hunterston Nuclear Power Station in Ayrshire, I had to spend a long time trying to explain to the recruitment officer the ways in which National Certificate modules could be built up to gain equivalencies to Highers. This experience was repeated at several meetings of a forum on 'Understanding British Industry'.

[6] See Matheson & Matheson (1998) for more on cultural imperialism in English-Scottish relations.

[7] At its outset at the end of the nineteenth century, *Kailyardism* was a popular literary style which celebrated the picturesque rusticity of the Scottish Lowlands wherein there was little but bucolic intrigues and small-minded village jealousies. The essential characteristics of Kailyard are humility, modesty, piety, honesty, poverty, perspicacity and cunning. In Scots, Kailyard means 'cabbage patch' and

this image neatly represents the narrow-minded, backward-looking nature of Kailyard novels. They were associated with, *inter alia*, the works of J.M. Barrie.

[8] Almost one-third of Scottish higher education is offered in further education colleges (*The Times Higher Education Supplement*, 21 August 1998).

[9] In addressing the House of Commons in the debate surrounding the Bill which would become the 1988 Education Reform Act, Kenneth Baker referred to improving the British education system. It does not inspire much faith when the Secretary of State for Education does not know for which education he is responsible.

## References

Anderson, R.D. (1983) *Educational Opportunity in Victorian Scotland*. Oxford: Clarendon Press.

Archer, M. (1979) *Social Origins of Education Systems*. London: Sage.

Bell, R. & Grant, N. (1974) *A Mythology of British Education*. St Albans: Panther.

Bell, R. & Grant, N. (1977) *Patterns of Education in the British Isles*. London: Allen & Unwin.

Benn, C. & Chitty, C. (1997) *Thirty Years On*. Harmondsworth: Penguin.

Breitenbach, E., Brown, A. & Myers, F. (1998) Understanding Women in Scotland, *Feminist Review*, Spring, pp. 44–65.

Corbett, J. (1997) *Language and Scottish Literature*. Edinburgh: Edinburgh University Press.

*Daily Telegraph [The]* (1998) Universities Told to Make Entry Easier, 18 September.

Davie, G. (1961) *The Democratic Intellect*. Edinburgh: Edinburgh University Press.

Grant, N. (1997) Intercultural Education in the United Kingdom, in D. Woodrow, G.K. Verma, M.B. Rocha-Trindade, G. Campani & C. Bagley (Eds) *Intercultural Education: theories, policies, and practice*. Aldershot: Ashgate.

Grant, N. & Docherty, F.J. (1992) Language Policy and Education: some Scottish-Catalan comparisons, *Comparative Education*, 28, pp. 145–165.

Kay, B. (1986) *Scots – The Mither Tongue*. Edinburgh: Mainstream.

McClure, J.D. (1988) *Why Scots Matters*. Edinburgh: The Saltire Society.

McCrone, D. (1996) *Understanding Scotland: the sociology of a stateless nation*. London: Routledge.

McPherson, A. & Raffe, D. (1988) *Governing Education*. Edinburgh: Edinburgh University Press.

Matheson, D. (1992) Post-Compulsory Education in Suisse Romande. Glasgow University: unpublished PhD thesis.

Matheson, C. (1999) Access to Higher Education, in D. Matheson & I. Grosvenor (Eds) *An Introduction to the Study of Education*. London: David Fulton.

Matheson, C. & Matheson, D. (1998) Problématiques Régionales et Questions Linguistiques en Ecosse, in S. Perez (Ed.) *La Mosaïque Linguistique*. Paris: L'Harmattan.

Meighan, R. & Siraj-Blatchford, I. (1998) *A Sociology of Educating*. London: Cassell.

Montgomery, M. (1986) *An Introduction to Language and Society*. London: Routledge.

Nairn, T. (1977) *The Break-Up of Britain*. London: NLB.

Nairn, T. (1988) *The Enchanted Glass*. London: Hutchison Radius.

National Foundation for Educational Research (1998) *Patterns of Mathematics and Science Teaching in Lower Secondary in England and Ten Other Countries. Third International Mathematics and Science Study. First National Report: Part 2.* http://www.nfer.ac.uk

Osmond, J. (1988) *The Divided Kingdom.* London: Constable.

Semple, B. (1998) *What do International Comparative Studies tell us about the Performance of Scottish Pupils?* http://www.scre.ac.uk

Scottish Office Education and Industry Department (SOEID) (1994) *Provision for Gaelic Education in Scotland.* Edinburgh: SOEID.

Scottish Qualifications Authority (SQA) (1998) *Comparability Study of Scottish Qualifications and GCE Advanced Level.* Dalkeith: SQA.

SQA (1998) *The Structure of National Qualifications* (available at http://www.sqa.org.uk/higher-still)

*Thig a Theasag* (1995) Inbhir Nis: Comunn na Gàidhlig.

Third International Mathematics and Science Study (1998a) *The Primary School Years* http://wwwcsteep.bc.edu/TIMSS1/HiLightA.html

Third International Mathematics and Science Study (1998b) *The Middle School Years* http://wwwcsteep.bc.edu/TIMSS1/HiLightB.html

*The Times Higher Education Supplement* (1998)Mature Students SWAP Direction, 21 August.

University of the Highlands and Islands (UHI) (1996) 21 August.

White, J. (1996) Education and Nationality, *Journal of Philosophy and Education,* 30, pp. 327–343.

# Northern Ireland:
# education in a divided society

## SEAMUS DUNN

### Introduction and Context

The purpose of this chapter is to look at the system of education in Northern Ireland, and in particular at the effects on that system of 30 years of violence and conflict. Context is as always of great importance, so it is necessary to begin by trying to portray the general setting within which the themes and questions that are specific to Northern Ireland can be characterised and understood.[1]

There have been many debates about what the Northern Ireland conflict is really about: answers have included:

- *Religion* – Catholics versus Protestants and what are deemed to be corresponding life-styles;
- *Nationality and Identity* – Irish versus British – Nationalism versus Unionism;
- *Culture* and way of life – Gaelic versus British;
- *Post-imperialism* – Ireland was Britain's first and last colony;
- *Class* – although Marxist analyses are rarer nowadays.

These are not necessary alternatives, and it is possible to perceive degrees of truth in more than one of them: but the confusion that they represent arises from the fact that Northern Ireland is in many ways part of two states: that is, it is – or represents – the long historical overlap, or the intersection, between Britain and Ireland, and so there is a Janus-like quality in its public life that almost automatically makes for bad politics. One consequence is that much of the great corpus of writing and publications about Northern Ireland has been focused on politics – on attempts to define and set-out some form of political and constitutional structure that will square the circle. So we have endless discussions and plans about power-sharing, joint sovereignty, frameworks and inter-governmental arrangements, committee systems, rotations of authority, and so on, to the extent that we seem almost to have invented a new tortuous political vocabulary (Dunn & Dawson, 2000).

The problems however are real enough and arise from the need to create formal political institutions – such as parliamentary assemblies, courts, bureaucracies, a police force – that are acceptable and have an ascriptive legitimacy. The level of enthusiasm generated by the Good Friday Agreement (Northern Ireland Office, 1998) and the establishment in 1999 of a legislative executive was in proportion to the degree that they seemed for the first time to have achieved something like this.

However I want to argue that although political evolution and development are necessary and of immeasurable importance, politics alone cannot be sufficient if we are to achieve a peaceful and calm society in Northern Ireland (Dunn, 1995). The people who live in Northern Ireland are not just divided politically; a great many of them continue to live almost completely separated lives. At its worst they live in segregated communities, but even when this is not the case they live together separately, and do not know each other in any complex social and cultural way. (Doherty & Poole, 1995; Poole & Doherty, 1996). They attend different churches; they play or watch or support different games – or different teams; they belong to different clubs and societies; they go to different pubs – or at best to different parts of the same pub; their children go to different schools; they celebrate different holidays. Of course I exaggerate to make the point, but the point is nonetheless valid.

At institutional level there is little enthusiasm for generating real contact and shared knowledge. In the mainstream churches, for example, despite much rhetoric from the top, there is little joint or shared activity. This is true almost by definition, and without necessarily any malevolence, because the churches act as props to the separate cultures and the divided social structures (Morrow et al, 1991, 1994). Church halls are the locus of much social activity. And churches and church buildings are burned down with depressing regularity.

We have separate sporting cultures which remain divided and antagonistic even when the two sides are playing the same game (Sugden & Harvie, 1995): senior soccer matches can lead to riots, and travelling coaches can be stoned. But many do not and so we have Gaelic football and hurling vs. rugby and hockey. Those who manage these sporting organisations have displayed little acceptance of their own contribution to social separation or their responsibility for the society within which they live and prosper.

So one analysis of the problem is that living together separately, protecting and maximising individual understandings of the world – while hoping or assuming that institutional manifestations of these understandings have benign outcomes – is at least as important a problem as political change. And of course the educational system – which is our subject today – can also be seen as a force for separation and division. Schools are therefore very often the focus of hatred and they, like churches, are often burned down.

### Educational Context – Pre 1969

When the latest outbreak of violence began in Northern Ireland in about 1969, there were two large educational sectors in the region, one attended almost exclusively by Protestants and the other almost exclusively by Catholics. Right from the beginning, therefore, there has been a debate within Northern Ireland about the possible impact of this segregated education system on the conflict. Whatever the substantive differences between the education provided by the two systems, it became widely believed and argued that there was some sort of connection between the actual separation itself and the absence of an enabling community understanding and cohesion (Dunn, 1986). But first a little bit of history.

### History – Pre 1920

Education in Ireland has always been a political and cultural tool. A system of National schools was established in Ireland in 1831 by the London government. It was an attempt to provide non-denominational education and was openly and specifically designed as an instrument of social engineering. The Irish were to be civilised and made moral by learning, and the contents of the then national curriculum had clear social and political intentions. Specially designed school books contained short readings with titles like *On the Beauty and Loveliness of Virtue, Education Compared To Sculpture*, along with copy-books with maxims such as 'the good is the enemy of the best, doing nothing is doing ill' and 'property has its duties as well as its rights'.

However, despite the intention that the schools should be non-denominational, all the churches – supported by their politicians – fought tenaciously from the beginning for segregated religious schools and for managerial – that is clerical – control of education, and inevitably the churches won. This to skate over a long and often bitter struggle, but the fact that education was always in dispute, and that there never was a universal common school system in Ireland may well be a symbol of that lack of national or cultural unity that still persists (Dunn, 1990, 1993; Farren, 1995).

However, the consequence was that, when the jurisdiction that was Northern Ireland came into being in 1920, two systems of education quickly emerged, reflecting to a considerable extent what had been there before. Right from the beginning therefore the community at school was divided rigidly along religious lines (Akenson, 1973). In addition, and perhaps of equal if not more importance, the anomaly was established right from the start that Protestant schools were totally funded and Catholic schools were very much less so. The consequence of this are obvious both in the material sense of placing a burden on Catholic parents and on the Catholic community, and on ensuring a lower quality of educational provision (although not, it is claimed, a lower educational quality); but also in the part it played in supporting and encouraging a sense of grievance, anger and discrimination. This latter consequence contributes still to the sense of anger and injustice in many Catholics in Northern Ireland, even now when there is equity of provision. These differential levels of funding were both overt and legal; but there were also covert and hidden dimensions protected by a complex and impenetrable system of educational payments. These last underpayments to the Catholic schools were revealed by researchers only in 1991 and led to a transparent and equitable system for the first time (Cormack et al, 1992).

So, skipping very rapidly over a very complex historical story, it is safe to say that when the current troubles began in 1969 there were two separate and distinct school systems in Northern Ireland, *de facto* Catholic and Protestant, although the Protestant system was *de jure* a state system.

### The Current System

However this dual system was and is not the whole story. The distinctive characteristic of the education system in Northern Ireland is segregation. It is segregated by religion in that most children attend predominantly Protestant schools or Catholic schools; by ability (which closely parallels social background) in that a selection system operates at age 11; and often by gender (particularly in second level education where a quarter of the secondary schools and almost half of all grammar schools are single sex).

All this endless subdivision takes place in a system that is relatively small. Statutory education encompasses approximately 350,000 children within 970 primary, 166 secondary and 70 grammar schools. One of the outcomes of this high degree of fragmentation combined with the small population and rural nature of Northern Ireland is that there are many small and very small schools. Primary schools with only 2 or 3 teachers and less than 70 pupils are still common.

The system is administered by a Department of Education and five local authorities (known as Education and Library Boards). There also exists a statutory Council for Catholic Maintained Schools and a body called the Northern Ireland Council for Integrated Education (NICIE) to co-ordinate the development of a small but growing number of religiously integrated schools. The education system also includes 8 Irish language schools, of which three receive grant-aid from government, and 10 independent Christian schools associated with the Free Presbyterian Church which do not receive government funds.

### The System Challenged

In the period between the 1920s and the 1970s, therefore, education acted mainly as a reflection of the more general society. The deep divisions between the two major traditions (Catholic/nationalist/Irish and Protestant/unionist/British) were accurately mirrored in this dual or separated education system. Since the outbreak of political violence in 1969, however, this traditional pattern has been challenged.

When questions about the role of separate schools were initially posed in the early 1970s it was very difficult to find any evidence to prove that damage was caused by separation, or that increased contact would have tangible benefits, and indeed it is still hard to produce clear evaluation data. But in a situation of severe violence, where a complete breakdown of social structures seemed close, there was a widespread, almost intuitive, belief that segregated education must play a part in perpetuating divisions. Some tangential support for such instinctive reactions was provided by the range of surveys carried out during this period (Cairns et al, 1993) which indicated how little young people from each community knew about their counterparts, and how few opportunities there were for meetings and contact. For example, while pupils in both types of schools often studied world religions such as Buddhism or Islam, they were very unlikely to study the religion of their nearest neighbours.

In the past three decades there has been more and more emphasis on how schools take account of the more general conflict and violence in the society. The result has been the introduction of a range of initiatives, including legislation, that define a more prominent role for schools in the improvement of relations between the two main religious and cultural communities in Northern Ireland. In broad terms these initiatives support interventions in both the process of education (through curriculum reforms and associated inter-group contact) and the structure of education (through consideration of equity issues between existing schools and support for the creation of new, integrated schools). These will now be described under the two more general headings of 'Education for Mutual Understanding' or EMU and 'Integrated Education' (Dunn, 1991).

## School Links and Cross Community Contact

The first research to examine the two segregated school systems (called Schools Apart) was carried out in 1975 (Darby et al, 1977; Murray, 1985). At that time little was known about the two school systems, and the research attempted to understand the ways in which they were different, to ask was there much cross-over of pupils between them, and how did their avowed religious character influence their daily work: that is the intention was to try to give a meaning to the much-quoted notion of individual school ethos, a notion always used as a justification by protagonists of separation and especially by the churches. The results suggested, among other things, that there was a genuinely segregated system, that is that there was little evidence of any significant level of crossover or interaction between the two sectors but that in almost all the publicly measurable ways, few obvious differences could be found.

The findings also suggested that the development of widespread integrated education was unlikely in the foreseeable future, although some argued that contacts between the two systems were strong enough to counteract the effects of segregation. So a second study set out to measure the amount of contact, of a sustained and important character, that actually existed between Catholic and Protestant schools (Dunn et al, 1984). The results of this suggested that very little contact existed between the two systems despite quite extravagant claims – from churches and others – of contact and cooperation between the two sectors.

At about the same time a number of experiments emerged that wished to find ways of linking schools and generating contact and friendship patterns among the pupils. Some of these had a religious dimension, some were more widely curricular, some were to do with joint activities such as sport or drama. These were fragmentary, individual, disconnected and voluntary, but they formed part of a movement that set out intentionally to generate ways whereby schools and pupils might work more closely together across the religious separation (Northern Ireland Council for Educational Development, 1988).

The Department of Education and government ministers were, to begin with, hesitant and cautious about suggestions that schools should be involved with community relations issues. Eventually this too began to change, and perhaps the most important influence on this change was not educational at all. The direct rule administration in Northern Ireland – unable to secure either a decisive military breakthrough or an internal political accommodation – began to turn its attention to social and economic initiatives. Following what has come to be referred to as 'the civil society approach' policies were initiated to try to increase equity in areas such as employment and housing and to encourage cross community co-operation at local level. This was reflected in legislation such as the Fair Employment Act and in the establishment of bodies such as the Community Relations Council, and the Central Community Relations Unit. Encouraging the tentative developments in educational co-operation fitted such an agenda well, and was relatively uncontroversial at the broader political level (Gallagher, 1992, 1995).

## Education for Mutual Understanding(EMU)

The result was that various levels of official support emerged and lead to the creation of ideas about what eventually came to be called EMU. In 1987 the Department of Education introduced a scheme that provided annual financial resources to encourage all schools in Northern Ireland to become involved in inter-school contact across the Catholic and Protestant religious divide (Northern Ireland, Department of Education, 1987, 1991). Participation in the scheme has increased annually and recent figures indicate that almost a third of primary schools and over a half of post-primary schools are now involved in some form of inter-school contact which brings Catholic and Protestant pupils together. However inter-school contact of this sort has never been seen as mandatory for the simple reason that in some places it would place children and their teachers in physical danger: it is however an optional strategy that teachers are encouraged to use.

Finally these ideas were made official government policy in the 'Education Reform (Northern Ireland) Order (1989)' which specifies that two 'cross-curricular themes' related to the issue of community relations be included in the Northern Ireland Curriculum. These are called *Education for Mutual Understanding* (1992a) and *Cultural Heritage* (1992b).

The statutory requirement to include these themes in the curriculum of all schools took effect from 1992 and the Northern Ireland Curriculum Council produced guidance material which supports the definition that, 'Education for Mutual Understanding is about self-respect, and respect for others, and the improvement of relationships between people of differing cultural traditions'. The aims and objectives state that as an integral part of their education the themes should enable pupils 'to learn to respect and value themselves and others; to appreciate the interdependence of people within society; to know about and understand what is shared as well as what is different about their cultural traditions; and to appreciate how conflict may be handled in non-violent ways' (Northern Ireland Curriculum Council 1990, 1992a,b).

There was to be no direct assessment of individual pupils as part of EMU. It was envisaged that its aims and objectives would form an integral part of programmes of study in all subjects. However it has become clear that for many schools the aims are being communicated – less formally – by the nature of relationships within the schools, and between the school and the wider community. In this sense many schools claim that the aims of EMU are implicit in their whole-school ethos.

All of this is still relatively new and there has not as yet been much research on effectiveness. In addition, much of the change has taken place in the context of the wider set of government-imposed educational changes introduced during the past 20 years. These relate to a more managerial, measurable and accountable system, including a national curriculum and attempts to improve efficiency and raise standards. In Northern Ireland, as in the rest of the UK, the emphasis during the 1990s has been on measuring pupil performance as an indicator of the success of schools and teachers. As a result published examination results and league tables have become important public measures of relative merit, and indeed such data has been particularly significant in a system still heavily influenced by the retention of selection by ability at the age of 11 and sharp distinctions in status between 'academic' grammar schools and secondary schools.

These more general concerns have meant that progress in establishing EMU as an integral part of the new statutory curriculum has been hindered by a combination of features – exclusion from formal assessment, integration into existing subjects and optional cross community contact. In addition, some teachers view EMU with suspicion, and those with strong political or religious views perceive it as politically motivated. The result has been that in many schools the subject has limited priority and relatively low status. The little evaluative research that has been done confirms that the inclusion of EMU in the statutory curriculum was largely unanticipated, with little training of teachers and a dearth of suitable curriculum ideas and materials (Smith & Robinson, 1992a,b, 1996). The notion of a cross-curricular theme is not always easily transformed into classroom materials and activities, and much of the work emerges from values-related subjects such as English literature, history, religious education and general or social studies. More universal themes such as gender relations, human rights, values, democracy, citizenship and ethnic diversity, have been increasingly emphasised as EMU becomes interpreted by a larger number of teachers (Montgomery & Smith, 1997). In addition many schools rely heavily on a strategy that focuses narrowly on generating more inter-school contact between Catholic and Protestant pupils, such as trips to the theatre, without always a lot of context. Finally, each school is expected to develop an EMU policy, and to appoint an EMU coordinator; but unless there is someone already involved and enthusiastic on the staff, the task of co-ordinator may not appear attractive and is often given to someone with limited interest and/or seniority.

The most pressing issue in the promotion of EMU is the need for a comprehensive plan of teacher training and the provision of support in relation to issues such as teaching controversial issues and dealing with contested matters especially historical questions.

## Integrated Schools

The second important form of change that has been taking place, essentially outside the existing segregated system, is the creation of Integrated Schools. These are schools that have been initiated by groups of parents working together to establish new institutions that are jointly managed and staffed on a cross-community basis. The aim of the integrated schools is that they should be attended by children from both Protestant and Catholic backgrounds, and should be open to children from other religious backgrounds and to children from backgrounds where there are no religious beliefs at all. In practice the schools are Christian in character and the founders, parents, teachers and managers have developed workable procedures for the teaching of religion (Wilson & Dunn, 1989; Dunn, 1989).

All along it has been recognised that it was most unlikely that the Catholic and Protestant schools would simply disappear or become integrated very quickly: so it was accepted that the majority of pupils would continue to be educated within the existing separated system. In addition the conservative political and religious power-bases within the society were, almost without exception, opposed to integrated schools – either overtly, like the Catholic Church, or more covertly, like most of the Protestant Churches.

Despite the high levels of suspicion and opposition, it could be argued that the most dramatic development in education in Northern Ireland over the past twenty years has been the creation of the integrated schools. The movement began in 1974 when a group called All Children Together (ACT) was established, composed of parents in favour of children being educated together. This organisation opened up the arguments, promoted discussion and debate and allowed various strategies for the generation of change to be tested. Eventually some parents within ACT decided to establish a new school that would exemplify their commitment to integrated education and the first planned, integrated school, Lagan College, was established in Belfast in 1981. This was followed by the opening of three further integrated schools in Belfast in 1985 and a pattern was established whereby at least one new integrated school has been established in Northern Ireland every year since. Much of the funding for these schools had, to begin with, to be raised from voluntary and charitable sources (Moffat, 1993).

The opening of each new school attracted international media attention and was widely presented as a rare 'good news' story from Northern Ireland. Against this background it became more difficult to attack integrated education directly and pressure built up for some form of official recognition and support. The Department of Education remained cautious, but by the late 1980s a recognised pattern had been established by which once an integrated school had been in operation for a few years, initially about four years, later one or two, and was attracting a steady and apparently sustainable enrolment, government took over financial responsibility.

Finally in 1989, a new Education Reform Order provided – for the first time – an official basis for support of integrated education. The Department of Education was given responsibility to 'encourage' the development of integrated schools where there was clear parental demand for such provision. At the same time it was recognised that there might be several ways of achieving this. Where parent groups were involved in establishing a new 'green field site' integrated school, funding could be provided as soon as the school opened if the department was satisfied that the school had a viable initial enrolment, from both sides of the community, acceptable premises and the prospect of sustained growth. In addition mechanism were put in place to allow existing schools to 'transform' themselves into integrated schools with the approval of the parents and governors. In the case of both new foundations and transformations, however, the details of procedure and the definition of criteria were not always precise or clear and within a few years this was to have some repercussions.

Perhaps not surprisingly the integrated schools remain a subject of disapproval by many within the community, especially from the Catholic church. Anxieties are also frequently voiced by teachers in the existing schools who believed that the growth of integrated schools poses a threat to the viability of existing schools and to the employment of teachers. Such fears are linked to the rapid expansion of integrated education and its long term implications. Particularly important from a government policy perspective – especially in relation to financial planning – has been the significant growth in the number of new secondary integrated schools – which are expensive.

A number of factors have contributed to this growth, of which the most obvious is the change in financial provision linked to the 1989 reforms. Whilst the possibility of government support for a school from the day it opened was clearly a major boost, the expansion of integrated secondary provision owed at least as much to forces within the movement for integrated education. As pupils who had attended the 'first wave' primary schools reached the age of eleven, and their parents were faced with choosing a suitable secondary school, it was inevitable that many of them would want their children to continue to be educated in an integrated environment.

Although the integrated sector remains comparatively small, its growth has been steady and successful (Northern Ireland Council for Integrated Education, 1992a,b, 1993, 1994, 1996, 1997). At the beginning of this 1998/99 school year Lagan College had over 1,000 students on its roll, and there are now 43 integrated schools in Northern Ireland made up as shown in Table I.

| | Total number of schools | Primary schools | Pupils in primary schools | Secondary schools | Pupils in secondary schools | Total pupils |
|---|---|---|---|---|---|---|
| All schools | 1,206 | 970 | 186,400 | 236 | 151,600 | 338,000 |
| Integrated schools | 43 | 26 | 4,414 | 17 | 6,164 | 10,578 |
| Percentages | 3.6 | 0.3 | 2.4 | 7.2 | 4.1 | 3.1 |

Table I. Northern Ireland school statistics.

The Education Reform (Northern Ireland) Order, 1989, included a number of provisions for the encouragement of integrated schools: these included the creation of a procedure for funding them, a mechanism to enable the transformation of existing schools into integrated schools, and placed a statutory responsibility on government to support and promote integrated education. It also facilitated the creation of central organising council called the Northern Ireland Council for Integrated Education (NICIE).

Despite the strides that have been made within the past two decades, integrated education is still in its infancy and the number of schools is limited. Currently the movement for integrated education faces difficult strategic issues concerning further development at secondary level within the competitive climate of a selective education system, and at a time of government financial constraint on capital development. The introduction of a policy of 'open enrolment' may also pose difficulties for the schools in terms of maintaining pupil enrolments which draw from both cultural traditions in equal proportions. It will only be possible to judge what the eventual level of uptake will be once a system of integrated schools becomes established on a more widespread basis.

## Note

[1] The best available analyses of the research literature are J. Whyte (1990) *Interpreting Northern Ireland* and Joseph Ruane & Jennifer Todd (1996) *The Dynamics of Conflict in Northern Ireland.*

## References

Akenson, D.H. (1973) *Education and Enmity: the control of schooling in Northern Ireland, 1920–50.* Newton Abbot: David & Charles.

Cairns, E., Dunn, S. & Giles, M. (1993) Surveys of Integrated Education in Northern Ireland: a review, in R. Osborne, R. Cormack & A. Gallagher (Eds) *After the Reforms: education and policy in Northern Ireland.* Aldershot: Avebury.

Cormack, R., Gallagher, A., Murray, D. & Osborne, R. (1992) *Curriculum, Access to Grammar Schools and the Financing of Schools, Seventeenth Report of the Standing Advisory Commission on Human Rights, Report for 1991–1992,* pp. 141–147. London: HMSO.

Darby, J., Batts, D., Dunn, S., Harris, J. & Farren, S. (1977) *Education and Community in Northern Ireland, Schools Apart?* Coleraine: University of Ulster.

Doherty, P. & Poole, M.A. (1995) *Ethnic Residential Segregation in Belfast.* Coleraine: Centre for the Study of Conflict, University of Ulster.

Dunn, S. (1986) The Role of Education in the Northern Ireland Conflict, *Oxford Review of Education,* 12, pp. 233–242.

Dunn, S. (1989) Integrated Schools in Northern Ireland, *Oxford Review of Education,* 15, pp. 121–127.

Dunn, S. (1990) *A History of Education in Northern Ireland Since 1920, Fifteenth Report of The Standing Advisory Commission on Human Rights, Northern Ireland,* Appendix B, pp. 49–96. London: HMSO.

Dunn, S. (1991) The Social Context of Education in Northern Ireland, *European Journal of Education,* 26, pp. 179–190.

Dunn, S. (1993) *The Common School.* Coleraine: Centre for the Study of Conflict, University of Ulster.

Dunn, S. (Ed.) (1995) *Facets of the Conflict in Northern Ireland.* London: Macmillan, St Martin's Press.

Dunn, S., Darby, J. & Mullan, K. (1984) *Schools Together?* Coleraine: Centre for the Study of Conflict, University of Ulster.

Dunn, S. & Dawson, H. (2000) *A Companion to the Conflict in Northern Ireland.* Lampeter: Edwin Mellen.

Farren, S. (1995) *The Politics of Irish Education, 1920–1965.* Belfast: Institute of Irish Studies, The Queen's University of Belfast.

Gallagher, A.M. (1992) Community Relations, in G. Robinson & P. Stringer (Eds) *Social Attitudes in Northern Ireland.* Belfast: Blackstaff Press.

Gallagher, A.M. (1995) *Majority Minority Review 1. Education in a Divided Society.* Coleraine: Centre for the Study of Conflict, University of Ulster.

Moffat, C. (1993) *Education Together for a Change. Integrated Education and Community Relations in Northern Ireland.* Belfast: Fortnight Educational Trust.

Morrow, D., Birrell, D., Greer, J. & O'Keeffe, T. (1991, 1994) *The Churches and Inter-community Relationships.* Coleraine: Centre for the Study of Conflict, University of Ulster.

Murray, D. (1985) *Worlds Apart. Segregated Schools in Northern Ireland.* Belfast: Appletree Press.

HMSO (1989) *Education Reform (NI) Order.* Belfast: Her Majesty's Stationery Office.

Northern Ireland Council for Educational Development (NICED) (1988) *Education for Mutual Understanding: a guide.* Belfast: NICED.

Northern Ireland Council for Integrated Education (NICIE) (1992a) *The Growth of Integrated Education: an Outline.* Belfast: NICIE.

NICIE (1992b, 1993) *Annual Reports.* Belfast: NICIE.

NICIE (1994) *Annual Report, 1993/1994.* Belfast: NICIE.

NICIE (1996) *Annual Report, 1995/1996.* Belfast: NICIE.

NICIE (1997) *Developments in Integrated Education.* Belfast: NICIE.

Northern Ireland Curriculum Council (NICC) (1990) *Cross-curricular Themes – Guidance Materials.* Belfast: NICC.

NICC (1992a) Education for Mutual Understanding: a cross-curricular theme, Belfast: NICC.

NICC (1992b) *Cultural heritage: a Cross-curricular theme.* Belfast: NICC.

Northern Ireland, Department of Education (DENI) (1987, 1991) *The Cross Community Contact Scheme.* Bangor: DENI Circular.

Poole, M.A. & Doherty, P. (1996) *Ethnic Residential Segregation in Northern Ireland.* Coleraine: Centre for the Study of Conflict, University of Ulster.

Ruane, J. & Todd, J. (1996) *The Dynamics of Conflict in Northern Ireland.* Cambridge: Cambridge University Press.

Smith, A. & Robinson, A. (1992a) *Education for Mutual Understanding: perceptions and policy.* Coleraine: Centre for the Study of Conflict, University of Ulster.

Smith, A. & Robinson, A. (1992b) *EMU in Transition. Report of a Conference on Education for Mutual Understanding.* Coleraine: Centre for the Study of Conflict, University of Ulster.

Smith, A. & Robinson, A. (1996) *Education for Mutual Understanding: the initial statutory years.* Coleraine: Centre for the Study of Conflict, University of Ulster.

Sugden, J. & Harvie, S. (1995) *Sport and Community in Northern Ireland.* Coleraine: Centre for the Study of Conflict, University of Ulster.

Wilson, D. & Dunn, S. (1989) *Integrated Education: information for parents.* Coleraine: Centre for the Study of Conflict, University of Ulster.

Whyte, J. (1990) *Interpreting Northern Ireland.* Oxford: Clarendon Press.

# Notes on Contributors

**SEAMUS DUNN** is Professor of Conflict Studies at the University of Ulster in Coleraine, Northern Ireland. He is Director of the Centre for the Study of Conflict and has published widely on conflict, and on the role of education in divided societies.

**STEPHEN GORARD** is a Senior Lecturer at the School of Social Sciences, University of Wales, Cardiff. His current research programme is funded by the ESRC ('Measuring Markets: the case of the Education Reform Act 1988), the National Assembly for Wales ('Lifelong Learning Targets: a research review'), the QCA for Wales ('Examining the Differential Attainment of Boys and Girls at School'), and the Spencer Foundation of the USA ('The Role of Technology in Widening Educational Participation'). He has also written widely on the process of school choice, school effectiveness, patterns of lifelong learning, and the relationship between education and the economy.

**CATHY HOWIESON** is Senior Research Fellow at the Centre for Educational Sociology in the University of Edinburgh. Her research interests include: secondary and post-secondary education and training systems; the relationship between general and vocational education and training; and young people's transitions. Recent publications include 'Using the Youth Cohort Study to Analyse the Outcomes of Careers Education and Guidance' (DfEE, 1996), 'Unifying Academic and Vocational Education: the state of the debate in England and Scotland' (*Journal of Education and Work*, 1997) and 'Careers Education' (in *Scottish Education*, ed. T. Bryce & W. Humes, 1999).

**DAVID MATHESON** was born and raised in Glasgow. He taught in Scotland, Spain and Switzerland before joining the staff at University College Northampton where he is Course Leader on the Education Studies course as well as running the Comparative Education M.Ed class in Glasgow University. He has published on the themes of lifelong education, culture and identity, and Scottish education.

**DAVID RAFFE** is Professor of Sociology of Education and Director of the Centre for Educational Sociology at the University of Edinburgh, where he has worked since 1975. He has research interests in secondary and post-secondary education and training and in transitions in youth. His current projects include a 'home international' comparison of 14–19 education systems in the United Kingdom, a comparison of the transition from education to work in European countries, analyses of the Scottish School Leavers Survey and a study of pos-16 policy changes in Scotland.

**KEN SPOURS** is a Lecturer in the Lifelong Learning Group at the Institute of Education, University of London. His main research interests lie in the areas of qualifications reform and the development of government policy in post-compulsory education and training. Ken is currently co-directing a national research project on institutional responses to 'Qualifying for Success' funded by the Nuffield Foundation. His recent publications include a co-authored book *New Labour's Educational Agenda: issues and policies for education and training from 14+* (Kogan Page, 1999).

**MICHAEL YOUNG** is Professor of Education at the Institute of Education, University of London. His main research interests are in comparative and sociological aspects of the curriculum for post-compulsory education and training and the changing role of qualifications. His most recent book was *The Curriculum of the Future* (Falmer Press, 1999).